The 2016 UEA Undergraduate Creative Writing Anthology

UNDERTOW

egg b•x   University of East Anglia

UNDERTOW

First published by Egg Box Publishing 2016

International ©2016 retained
by individual authors.

A CIP record for this book is available
from the British Library.

Undergrowth is typeset in Adobe Garamond.
Titles are set in GT Cinetype.

Printed and bound in the
UK by Imprint Digital.

Designed and typeset by Sean Purdy.

Proofread by Imogen Lees.

Distributed by Central Books.

ISBN: 978-0-9932962-6-0

Editor's note

U*ndertow* is the third incarnation of the University of East Anglia's
undergraduate anthology. We are confident that in this anthology
you will discover some of the best work by UEA undergraduate students.
With pieces concerning everything from aliens in Birmingham and the
struggle for racial justice to a hotel minibar and children of the sea, *Undertow*
is filled with refreshing and vital writing that we are proud to present.

We would like to thank Philip Langeskov, Nathan Hamilton at Egg Box
Publishing, and Sean Purdy for their assistance and support. We would
also like to thank the following students who assisted with the selection
and editing of work:

Erin Bashford, Harry Bennett, Alice Clarke, Grace Fothergill, Sarah
Hudis, Ava McKenzie Welch, Sarra Said-Wardell, Jay Slayton-Joslin,
Stoyo Stoev, Marion Weaver and Nathaniel Woo.

We would also like to say a special thanks to Peter Liss from the
School of Environmental Sciences for providing the introduction this
year. Our brief exchanges on the architecture at UEA, getting people
interested in environmental sciences (no matter how limited their skills in
mathematics), and of course the ocean's undertow, have been inspirational.

We hope you enjoy being caught in the *Undertow*.

THE EDITORIAL TEAM
Anastasia Dukakis, Francesca Kritikos and Jessica Rhodes

Contents

UNDERTOW

Peter Liss

Introduction

WAS RATHER SURPRISED to be approached to write this introduction. I
am someone who enjoys a non-professional interaction with literature –
reading modern novels, books that show how history can explain the
way the world is now – but who has spent his professional life reading
non-fiction, researching the oceans from a natural science perspective. On
further reflection, however, I began to see several connections between
where myself and the readers of this anthology are coming from.

Perhaps first I need to say a few words about my research area and
then the connections to *Undertow* will perhaps become more apparent. I
research the ways in which the oceans and the atmosphere interact and more
specifically how gases flow between the two domains in both directions.
So, for example, the greenhouse gas carbon dioxide exchanges between
ocean and atmosphere and vice versa in a complex series of flows that vary
both seasonally and geographically in the natural situation: the net effect,
uptake (or release) being the resultant of these flows. In passing we can note
that with man's activities in burning large amounts of hydrocarbon fuels
and changing land use an extra increment of carbon dioxide is injected
into the atmosphere, a significant fraction of which is taken up by the
oceans (about 35%). If the oceans did not provide this "service" to us then
the globe would be significantly warmer than it is today. Understanding
these natural and man-induced flows is vital if we are correctly to predict
future climate change owing to continued release of carbon dioxide. This
single example (there are many others) should, hopefully, be sufficient to
show how natural flows studied by environmental scientists could be of
relevance to the poems and prose pieces in this book.

Let us turn now to interpreting the concept of "undertow", which is the
flow of water beneath the surface in the opposite direction to the surface
flow. An obvious example is on the seashore, where the waves crashing on

the sand or shingle as the beach shallows are the manifestation of surface flow. On the other hand, the undertow (or reverse flow) is the movement of water and suspended sediment in the opposite direction down the beach. Together these two flows control the net movement of material, and therefore whether the beach is accreting or eroding. An obvious manifestation is the beautiful patterns of sand ripples seen on many beaches. Something else to note is that the undertow is visually less dramatic than the crashing waves carrying water and particles up the beach. But although less obvious, the effect is none the less vital in shaping the slope of the beach and the ripple pattern as a manifestation of the net effect of the up and down flows. Maybe this more subtle aspect of undertow will be reflected in literary form, in these writers, as we bear witness to these their formative works.

Turning away from the seashore we can develop the ideas of flows and their interaction to our own campus here at UEA. The innovative and thoughtful design of the original architect, Denys Lasdun, gave us a circulation system where people are separated from vehicles and pedestrians have their own flowing system of the walkways. These link the various schools and services. It seems clear that the architect intended to aid the interaction between disciplines, and how well this works in practice you can judge from your own experience; but it clearly presents possibilities that could perhaps be better exploited. However, it is the mixing of the flows and the resulting exchange of ideas from which the new insights and discoveries emerge and will do so even more in the future. At UEA we have a physical infrastructure that is conducive to this. It complements the founding ideas of the university to take a novel cross- and inter-disciplinary approach to both teaching and research, which is still a distinctive feature today.

The pieces in this anthology are striking in their originality in form and content. I have found them very stimulating and a great read. I hope you do too.

PETER LISS
School of Environmental Sciences
University of East Anglia

Blythe Aimson

La Grande Mère[1]
(III The Empress)

Me,
wide-eyed, hiding
behind crocheted cloth,
watching two figures
at the kitchen table –

teapot and Tarot between them,
esoteric is domestic as
the Empress,
my Mother,
shuffles, reshuffles
draws
     draws
          draws
flicks through pages
recurrence making meaning
offering interpretations
that collide with
how was your appointment?
what did so-and-so say?

Years later, she says
you might be a changeling
child.
Midnight, midsummer
in the woods is the right place
to be stolen.
Still she shuffles,

lays out cards in my name –
ten of swords
       a pentacle
           a queen appears
and even as a changeling,
I am still
hers.

1: (After the French revolution, Royal cards were often stripped of their titles. III
The Empress was known as *La Grande Mère*, meaning 'The Great Mother',
rather than 'The Grandmother')
Fate and Fortune, Brian Innes, page 288

Erin Bashford

One man's moon

ONE THING OF WHICH GREGORY PEARLMAN was certain was his innate ability to gamble successfully. Whether he concentrated on the throw or simply wagered with his back to the table, he always won. It was something that he could not control, that he did not know the origin of, but it was a skill that had been with him since his first visit to a casino.

This evening, however, he was unable to while away time spinning dice and picking cards. He was dotting a pen continuously on to his desk, slinking down in his chair when he noticed the nib had concaved and the wood dented. Now he had an excuse not to sign a form he really didn't want to sign – he had no pens.

Gregory refocused on the first sentence of the paper, his vision tilting and blurring every now and again. "Dear Mr. Pearlman, many congratulations on your promotion..." He inadvertently rolled his eyes. How many of these leaders would see his new job as a thing to congratulate?

In his peripheral vision he saw his broken pen spinning uncontrollably. He stopped it, slammed it on to the table, groaning at his lack of self-control.

The movement on his desk caused Gregory's temperamental vintage lamp to flicker uncontrollably, making reading papers difficult. While steadying the desk and the lamp, Pearlman pushed his feet into the floor, pressing the papers on to the desk with an equal amount of force, and digested the words he should have digested days ago.

"However, it has come to my knowledge... we must attack... you are restraining... we are resorting to... you must reply immediately... action *will* be taken... for the love of Fuar..."

It was just the same nonsense he had hoped to rise above since his latest promotion. He discarded the letter.

Rising, he turned to face the crystal window behind his desk. Both moons peered over the horizon, despite the sky retaining the blue of day.

NE THING OF WHICH GREGORY PEARLMAN was certain was his innate ability to gamble successfully. Whether he concentrated on the throw or simply wagered with his back to the table, he always won. It was something that he could not control, that he did not know the origin of, but it was a skill that had been with him since his first visit to a casino.

This evening, however, he was unable to while away time spinning dice and picking cards. He was dotting a pen continuously on to his desk, slinking down in his chair when he noticed the nib had concaved and the wood dented. Now he had an excuse not to sign a form he really didn't want to sign – he had no pens.

Gregory refocused on the first sentence of the paper, his vision tilting and blurring every now and again. "Dear Mr. Pearlman, many congratulations on your promotion..." He inadvertently rolled his eyes. How many of these leaders would see his new job as a thing to congratulate?

In his peripheral vision he saw his broken pen spinning uncontrollably. He stopped it, slammed it on to the table, groaning at his lack of self-control.

The movement on his desk caused Gregory's temperamental vintage lamp to flicker uncontrollably, making reading papers difficult. While steadying the desk and the lamp, Pearlman pushed his feet into the floor, pressing the papers on to the desk with an equal amount of force, and digested the words he should have digested days ago.

"However, it has come to my knowledge... we must attack... you are restraining... we are resorting to... you must reply immediately... action *will* be taken... for the love of Fuar..."

It was just the same nonsense he had hoped to rise above since his latest promotion. He discarded the letter.

Rising, he turned to face the crystal window behind his desk. Both moons peered over the horizon, despite the sky retaining the blue of day. No clouds littered the atmosphere this evening, only birds, aeroplanes, and the occasional teenager exerting archetypical rebellion by flying higher than the law allowed. Streetlights, factory lights, commercial lights and residential lights added to the urban ambience. Gregory futilely wondered how different the world would be if people would turn their power off when they no longer needed it. He would gaze over this same vista, but only see the silhouettes of concrete skyscrapers and both moons emanating their infinite light.

He scratched at his small beard. The foreboding nature of the letter worried him, although he would not admit that to himself. This office had not been his long enough to torment him.

Gregory collated the papers, clipping them together wonkily, and tucked them under his arm as he left the office. He left the light on.

*

Her dog's fur was invisible in the late snow. All day, Marita's petite frame had remained wracked with cold, shivers tormenting her; now, she fully believed that even her bones were quivering.

The orange moon on her left and the blue moon on her right were not supposed to be out this late, which, Marita assumed, was the reason for the day's polarised weather. In the morning it had been roasting and she had spent a few hours sunbathing. Almost immediately after midday, though, snow had begun falling and she had taken to catching flakes on her tongue.

Marita's dog, an uncharacteristically large Mittelspitz, rolled around in the snow, his pink tongue and black nose the only observable parts of him. He seemed in pure bliss, eyes closed, paws up, tail creating grooves in the settled flurry. She felt warmth pulsate through her, despite the frigidity of the air. Her entire face smiled on reflex, her emotion palpable, as she watched him enjoying himself for the first time in millennia.

Disrupting Marita's dog's play, a crash sounded behind her. She felt the tranquillity of the moment crack, and threw herself on her dog, covering him. She made it look like she was simply a tramp searching fruitlessly among bins for a scrap to eat – that was what she wanted. What she was.

"Look here, Lou," Marita heard a gravelly voice behind her. It was followed by a gnarled laugh. She refused to look.

"A straggler." The same voice spoke again. "What d'you reckon we should do with it?"

Marita found the silence that followed suffocating. The tips of her ears burned, and her heart thundered in her stomach. Her dog remained motionless underneath her, as they had practised many times before.

"Why are you out so late? Don't have a home to hide in?" A second, more high-pitched, character spoke.

Marita remained deathly silent while the men taunted her. Her back felt naked, despite the three jackets she had thrown over herself. Her skin was raised and prickled, her muscles tensed.

"Not gonna talk, sweetheart?" the second man spoke again. Marita's mind was white, empty. She dared not breathe.

"Come on, Lou. She ain't worth it. You're only an inch from being back in hell, remember?" Seeing nothing but the fabric of her outermost coat and her dog's fur, Marita listened raptly as the men plodded away.

Her dog let out a small whimper and Marita felt her heart crack. He sounded so desperate for change, so fraught for safety. She scrambled off him, brushing her taupe trousers with her fingers. Outside their alleyway was the thickness of silence.

The navy sky did not allow for much natural light. As a result of the premature night, Marita's abode of a dead-end alleyway was swathed in gloom, hiding her from interfering onlookers. Nightfall, especially early nightfall, was something she was tangibly grateful for. Only when she really squinted could she see her dog, curled up among discarded coats and blankets. She hastily hid him.

"Stay here and don't make a sound," she warned her dog, forcing herself to leave their cave. "I will be back very soon."

Marita stuck her hands into her pockets and emerged from her home, ensuring there were no passers-by on the usually empty street. It was clear. She kicked up snow as she walked away. It was oddly, almost unnervingly, quiet for this time of night. Usually, teenagers were lying about their ages, middle-aged women were hoping to be asked for ID, and businessmen were telling a mendacious story to their wives about why they would be out all evening. There were supposed to be shouts from houses, throbbing drumbeats from clubs, sirens from police cars.

Instead, there were only lights. Only the neon of billboards and muted lamps of living rooms showed that the city had life left.

*

Gregory slammed two coins on to the counter. "Give me the strongest thing you have," he ordered, without even looking at the barkeep. He took it back in one gulp, and, like clockwork, he waited for the alcohol to take effect. Yet it was only after his third drink that he actually felt his stress alleviate. That aggressive letter appeared a mere joke now. His laughter was like an orange bubble when he released it, resulting in a few odd glances from the two other men in the institution.

"Do you have anything that you wouldn't mind giving away for free?" Gregory heard a soft voice next to him, a voice that drifted into his tormented mind like a feather floating to Earth.

"Is stale milk all right?" The barman's sardonic question was met with a whimper.

"Tap water?" she almost begged. The undeniable desperation in her youthful voice made Gregory take his hand away from his temples and pay full attention to the conversation.

It was obvious that the girl was homeless. Her fingerless gloves and entirely brown outfit, complete with three jackets, was reminiscent of every other street-person in this city. They were *his* problem, according to the public. It was his fault there were so many without homes. He should help her.

"Here," Gregory pushed a coin across the bar. "Get some decent stuff. You don't know how much crap is in tap water."

The girl's response was cut off by a burning wave. A shock of heat pulsated around him, and his sight disappeared for one petrifying heartbeat. Gregory was thrown backwards; instinctively, he grabbed the girl by the shoulder and both of them crashed into the wall behind the bar. Bottles splintered, covering them both with liquids that seared their skin. The girl's raven hair was soaked with flammable spirits and her clothes stuck to her skin. Gregory watched in horror as she was knocked unconscious by a falling Jeroboam champagne bottle, and desperately hauled her backwards, away from the smashing glass that surrounded her. He found himself dragging the girl to a door that must have led to a storeroom. It swung open as he pushed against it.

The girl shook herself awake. When she had realised that the bar was on fire, she sprung up, but soon winced and clasped her hand to her scalp.

"What's happening?" Her shout was tinged with hysteria.

Meanwhile, Gregory had found an exit. "Here, come through here," he said, directing her with a hand on the small of her back. This bar, the ground floor of one of the tallest skyscrapers in the city, emerged on to another thriving street. People were screaming, crying.

Gregory glanced furtively around and saw that everything was encapsulated in an inferno, the whole city looking like the heart of a volcano and the sky poisoned with mushroom clouds. His stomach twisted painfully.

In the sky, only the blue moon remained, illuminated orange by the fires in his city.

Mathilda Beaumont Epstein

Little fish

IT ARRIVED THE WINTER I TURNED SEVEN, big and blue and strange like a spaceship, or a whale. I wasn't allowed to climb in it, this big swimming pool that had suddenly taken up residence in our bathroom. Like my mum's swollen belly, this was unknown territory, repulsive and fascinating. Sometimes, when everyone was sleeping, the house quiet, I would scramble into the empty pool. From the middle of its blue insides everything looked different; the bathroom transformed into a series of strange dark shapes. I would imagine it was my mum's belly and I was back inside it with the baby. I could see us as little fish, splashing around together. Once, my dad caught me sleeping in the pool. Sighing, he carried me back to bed, tucking me into the cool sheets.

"Not long to wait now, Ella," he whispered, the door closing softly behind him.

In the last weeks of my mother's pregnancy she could hardly move and her stomach seemed to fill the entire room. She would take my hand, guiding it gently across her stomach until I could feel kicking against my palm.

"The baby's trying to get out," she would say. I clung to her then, drinking in her scent of rosemary and greedily kissing her full on the lips.

We climbed to the top of Kite Hill, the day before the baby arrived. The wind whipped around us as if celebrating the sight of London stretched out far below us.

"I've had a thought," said my dad, his voice carried high into the air by the wind.

"Isn't it strange that the baby has literally no idea it's at the top of Kite Hill?—" My mum laughed.

"Very profound, John." My dad swung me down from the great height of his shoulders.

"What's profound?" I asked.

"I'm being serious, though." My dad ignored me, like he always did when he was excited by something. "'Isn't it crazy that it has no idea that there is an entire world outside your stomach? Imagine, like seriously imagine, what it would be like, to see the world again through completely fresh eyes."

I thought about it. It seemed so strange that it didn't know about simple things, like London and chocolate cake and how the leaves change to a deep orange in autumn. My mum smiled as she took my hand in hers and we started the long walk back down the hill.

That night I dreamed that I opened my mother's belly with a key and an ocean flooded out of it, a great wave sweeping me away. I felt myself drowning, the water seeping into my eyes and lungs, dragging me further and further downwards. I awoke suddenly. The short rasps of my breath echoed loudly in the quiet of my room. Clouded in sleep, I slipped out of bed. In the darkness the corridor seemed to stretch on infinitely. A light was shining through a crack in the bathroom door. I paused. A scream pierced through the night. I flung open the door. The light was shocking. My mum was in the pool, naked, her legs spread wide apart. Faceless doctors surrounded her and her eyes were black and wild. An arm grabbed me from behind, pulling me backwards so I was shrouded in the shadows of the corridor once again. My dad's face loomed out at me from the darkness.

"Go back to bed, Ella. The baby's coming." He picked me up, carrying me back to bed,

"Everything's fine." It took me a long time to get back to sleep.

The next morning I awoke with a start, hurtling down the stairs to find my grandfather sat alone at the kitchen table.

"Where's mum?" He looked at me. "And the baby?" He stood up, pulling me into a crushing embrace.

"Do you not have a hello for your Sabba?" He was a huge man, his body once strong and tall had sagged over the years, as if in disappointment that he had grown old. Despite living in England for more than half his life, he still had a stubborn Israeli accent.

"Where's mum?" I asked again. He smiled, but there was something guarded in his expression.

"Don't worry, Ella, Sabba is here. Your mother, she is in hospital with the baby and your father."

"But Dad said they'd be here." I felt hot tears starting to gather behind my eyes. "I want my mum." Sabba frowned.

"Today you are having a special day with Sabba. Are you not happy for this?" I felt a single tear drip pathetically down my face.

"But I want to see my mum." He reached out a large finger, firmly brushing the tear away. "Why are you crying? You will come and stay the night at my house tonight, yes? For a special treat I will make you hot chocolate. Come now, go and get your toothbrush and we will go." I opened my mouth to protest but he shook his head. "I will ask you only once." I did as I was told.

Sabba's house smelled like damp, and with only one small window, time seemed to drag on indefinitely with no separation between day and night. The television was always on, casting a clinical blue light over the small living room. Sabba seemed distracted, leaving me staring at the screen until it was time for bed, and then long past that, the animated, too-bright faces slowly blurring into one. I couldn't understand why they'd left me. Maybe it was a punishment. I thought about all the bad things I'd ever done and felt a knot of pain in my stomach. Sabba had bought me a box of chocolates and I ate them ravenously one after the other until I felt so sick I couldn't concentrate on anything and the knot went away.

"Time for bed." Sabba switched off the TV. "Did you eat all the chocolates, you naughty girl?" I nodded. "You will get fat if you're not careful. Now upstairs to bed. I love you very much. Your Daddy is coming to pick you up in the morning."

The sheets on Sabba's bed smelled sickly sweet, like honey left out in the sun. An African mask hung on the wall. I drifted in and out of sleep. I could feel something watching me. The mask. It opened its mouth slowly, its face morphing into a strange, twisted grimace. It had my mother's eyes. Black and pained, they looked straight at me, pleading for help. I squeezed my eyes shut, diving deep under the duvet until I was submerged in the safety of blackness. Slowly, something emerged from the depths of the watery darkness, pushing forcefully at the back of my brain. I let it in, allowing it to grow until I could feel nothing else. I hate the baby.

The next morning, my dad's familiar smell of smoke sent relief coursing through my body. He hugged me tightly.

"I'm sorry, Els," he said.

"You said you'd be there" – I could feel hot anger pushing to get out – "and you left me! You just left me on my own. Where's mum? I want to see mum!"

My dad looked at me.

"Els," his voice sounded strange. "Something has happened with the baby. Something that we weren't expecting." He picked at a bit of loose skin on his nail. "She's different from other babies." He paused for a second and a silence seemed to stretch out before us. He cleared his throat. "She has Down's syndrome." Down's syndrome. It sounded strange. "It means she won't learn things as quickly as other children." He paused again. "And it means she looks a bit different as well." I imagined a monster. "I know this is a lot to take in," said my dad, "but it's going to be OK. She's still a little baby and you have a sister, like you wanted.'" His smile didn't seem to reach his eyes.

"I just want to see mum." Dad nodded.

"Let's go home."

The baby's name was Nelly. I looked at her small body wrapped in layers of thick blankets and could think only of a package sent to the wrong address. I imagined another baby that looked just like me, abandoned alone in the hospital. I'd watched a nature programme with my dad once about cuckoos. Climbing into other bird's nests and killing their babies, they tricked the mum and dad birds into feeding them until they grew into ugly, great birds.

"Cuckoo!" I hissed at Nelly. She smirked, her mouth mean and puckered.

Routine became the only way to loosen the knot that had stubbornly tied itself to the depths of my belly. On the way to school I counted every lamppost I passed. At lunchtime I would go to the library, the shouts of the playground echoing faintly in the distance as I tried to read exactly three chapters before the bell. Failure was punished with a sharp tightening of the knot. Every night, I would creep downstairs to the kitchen and gorge myself on whatever food I could find. Sometimes nausea would make me stop, and I would go and sneak a look in Nelly's room. The sight of her face would only tighten the ever-present knot, forcing me to eat even more.

My body started to change, my belly expanding into rolls of fat that stretched over my jeans. Once, I overheard some girls discussing my swollen body in the toilets. I hid inside the cubicle, my face burning with shame. As I became physically bigger, I seemed only to grow more invisible.

One night, while standing on a chair to reach for a biscuit tin, high on the top shelf, I lost my balance. The whole shelf toppled down on me in an almighty crash. I lay where I fell, food littered around me like fallen leaves. I heard lights frantically being switched on and the panicked run of my Mum's footsteps down the stairs.

"Ella?" she screamed. "What the fuck is this?" I felt the knot inside me explode, rushing out through my mouth in a strangled sob. Tears streamed down my face until my body shook uncontrollably. My mum took me in her arms, her body warm and familiar against mine.

"It's my fault, mum," I sobbed.

"Shhh, darling. "What's your fault?"

"The Down's syndrome. Nelly has it because I was bad and I've been trying to make it better but I can't." My mum looked at me fiercely.

"Never think that, Els. It's not your fault. Nelly has Down's syndrome because things like that just happen. All we can do is accept and love her." I felt lighter. "I know that I haven't been the best mum to you since Nelly was born, but you have to know that I love you." She took my face in her hands and looked deep into my eyes. "But I love Nelly too, and she needs me." I nodded. "She needs you too, Els; she needs her sister." I felt a fresh wave of sobs threaten to overtake me. "But tomorrow, how about me and you go for a walk, just us? Would you like that?" I nodded. It wasn't my fault.

"Can we go to Kite Hill?" My mum smiled.

"Of course, darling. Now let's go back to sleep. And promise me, no more late-night eating."

She kissed me on the forehead, taking my hand as we went back to bed, leaving the mess of the kitchen behind us.

As I lay in bed, I still couldn't sleep, and I found myself, again, standing in Nelly's room. I looked down into her cot. To my surprise, she was staring straight back at me, awake and alert. I noticed, for the first time, that her eyes were a deep ocean blue. Her face spread into a smile, like a wave quietly breaking over a pebbled shore.

"Hello Nelly," I whispered.

Liza Blackman

The deck chairs

S ITTING ON A PLASTIC DECK CHAIR in 'Debbie's back garden eight weeks ago, I came to the shocking realisation that I 'hadn't been fully naked in front of Tom in more than four months. Four whole months! Not that we 'hadn't been having sex, of course – we both have our needs, after all – but for some reason I was never fully naked. He always got started right before I managed to get my bra off. Every time I'd be on my knees, prepped to go, teeth already cleaned, and right before I'd whip it off he'd be on me like a Grass-O-Matic 3000 lawnmower on a flower bed.

It kept me up at night thinking about it. I'd lay staring up at our stupidly low ceilings and shifting under the covers trying to puzzle it all out. I mean, it's hard enough to sleep with his arms and legs sprawled all over the place like a load of super-heated pool noodles, plus the constant drone of his cow in a meat grinder snores, but this made it completely impossible.

At first I figured, well, he's just eager, isn't he? Kids are off at uni, dog's finally kicked it, big old house all to our old selves and all that. But if that were the case, why was it only every few days we'd get down and dirty? Surely he'd be pulling on me every spare minute for a bit o'cheeky rough and tumble on the sofa, kitchen counter, Russian carpet, back porch and every other fixture we happened to be standing by at the time (my dodgy hip be damned)? And let me tell you, as a pair of farm owners in a town full of kids looking for work, we have a lot of spare minutes.

Then I realised. It's my tits. He doesn't like my tits any more. I know I'm getting on a bit, fifty three, I'm not the most spring of chickens... but, come on, they're perfectly reasonable tits! Now if it was my arse, I'd understand; the thing is practically dragging across the hardwood floors, but my tits are fine.

He can hardly talk, though. Every time he yanks off one of his blooming vest tops I'm greeted with the Nottingham Forest of back hair through my fingers like a cheese grater. Not to mention putting up with the nose-assaulting stench of Carol Blackwell's homemade mint, lavender and wood smoke aftershave that he routinely dowses himself in. Covers the smell of farm, my arse; the farm smells like a deep-fried Mars bar in comparison. I put up with all of this, day in day out (shag in shag out), and he can't handle some mild boob sag: pathetic.

Three weeks after I'd figured out Tom's reasoning I'm down the shops, chatting away to Debbie and telling her my tales of woe; ever the sweetheart, she's trying to come up with other ideas. So we wind up back on the deck chairs, a cold pint for each of us, and she says to me: "Fran, I'll tell you what it is. It's the bra. He loves the bra."

"He'd bloody better love the bra," I said. "Pinching that from Ann Summers was a right pain. Forty-five pounds for a bra? You're having a laugh, even if it does feel like a Spanish bloke's hands holding me up all day."

Then, insult to injury, we start going at it less and less. He's not even the last bloke to say he loved me, you know. The other week in Morrisons, I popped three pound sixty in David's charity box he does for Church and he says to me: "I tell you what, Franny, I really love ya sometimes." Bloody David. The boy is gay!

I'd always feared this'd happen. I'd get old, lose my looks and Tom would start trailing off after younger models. Look at me now: hair going grey, eyes going wrong and everything else going south. Fast. I look like an extra from the before scene of an anti-ageing commercial. Still haven't been to Greece, still haven't been on a yacht and the only affection I get is from Debbie (after a few too many) and the flipping homosexual community.

So I said enough is e-bloody-nough. I've put too much time, money and coffee into keeping our love life in check for a stupid bra to get in the way of my underappreciated bosom. So here I stand, Debbie at my side with a nice glass of white, making a point. Like Thelma and Louise without that suicide and murder business. The smoke smells like pleasant chemicals: sort of like if a Lush store caught fire, and the heat is just keeping off the beginnings of an autumn chill.

"Makes you feel a bit like a sixties feminists, don't it?"

Laughing, brains bordering on tipsy, we walk away from the small pile of burned bras and return to our deck chairs.

Callum Browne

The egg on the
hill that dreams

"SEE, THE THING YOU'VE GOT TO UNDERSTAND IS, we were desperate." The old woman let a thin whisper of smoke squeeze between her lips and stared deep into the fire. "Proper desperate, like. You youngsters don't know how good you've got it, with a meal every day, and shoes on your feet. Back in my day we had it proper rough."

The young girl next to her shivered and clutched her shoulders. Nights were always bitter up here on the hilltop, but it's where the sheep seemed most comfortable, and someone had to watch them. The old woman took another puff and shook a few clods of ash on to the grass.

"This was just after the big heat, so food was a bit on the rare side, like, but that wasn't the problem," she continued, fishing out her tobacco pouch. "People have been hungry before, they'll be hungry again. They're used to it. More or less. It was all the other stuff."

"What other stuff?" asked the young girl, looking at her over her shoulder. The old woman waved her hand.

"Well, you know," she said. "All that other stuff. All the cars had packed up and died, we couldn't keep the lights on for more than about an hour every night. My mum, your great grandma that is, couldn't even afford to run her iPhone anymore, with all the power shortages."

The young girl frowned. "What's an iPhone?"

Her grandmother paused and thought for a while. She couldn't entirely remember what an iPhone was, having been so young at the time, but somehow she suspected that "the thing we used to stick under the table leg to stop it wobbling" probably wouldn't do as an answer.

"It was a sort of electric brick," she said, finally, after much deliberation. The young girl nodded sagely. Everything had been electric in the old days. Apparently that had extended to building materials. "But that's not the point."

The old woman stuffed a small clump of tobacco into the mouth of her pipe and lit it with a match, shaking it out just before the flame reached her fingers.

"The point is, there were riots. All the time. Sometimes it was about the heat. Sometimes they were about whatever ponce was in charge, and someone thought their ponce was better and kicked up a fuss, and then their one turned out to be a bastard too. Sometimes it was even about the food, although that was usually on the days they couldn't think of anything else. But mostly, I remember it being about the power. Always about the power. Can't remember a week that went by without something getting burned down, or blown up." She smiled softly to herself. "Funny thing about a shortage. Can't get anything else for love nor money, but there always seems to be enough bombs to go around."

She stared into the fire again, while the sheep chewed lazily under the starless sky. The young girl watched her with wide eyes. After a minute or so, she cleared her throat.

"So what about the thinker?" she asked. "You said something about the thinker?"

"Hmmm?" Her grandmother looked back up at her. "Oh, yeah. Of course." She shuffled round slightly to face her, and crossed her legs, leaning forward so the moon sat above her like a full stop.

"Right, so shortages, riots, stuff blowing up, that's set the general scene type thing. So things were pretty bad, as you can imagine." She took another puff and let the smoke gutter upwards.

"And then along comes this woman," she went on, out of the corner of her mouth while she lit the pipe again. "One of the toffs, like: nice suit, nice hair, nice nails. And what she had, was a solution. And this was on all the screens, for that one hour a night we had them on, every last one, 'cos it had to be really. By this point everyone had pretty much given up. No one really believed that things were ever going to go back to normal, and definitely not 'cos of some toff. They weren't the ones starving, and they could have their screens on all the time, so why would they help?"

"So why did they?" The young girl watched a sheep in the distance as it licked its own hooves with an expression of intense curiosity, before ambling away. Apparently it was satisfied.

"Dunno, really. Probably a tax thing." The old woman sniffed and rubbed her nose. "But anyway, this toff, she went on all the screens, and she said that what we really needed was something called an AI. An 'artificial intelligence'."

"And that was the thinker?"

The old woman scowled and waved a hand. "Hold on, hold on; I'm getting to that. So another thing you need to understand is that an AI isn't just a big computer, although it was a big computer. An AI is alive. It does real, proper thinking. Not just a good impression of it, like most people do.

And this toff, she said it could fix *everything*, and I mean *everything*. All-seeing, all-knowing, all-powerful. It was going to fix the seas, stop the heat, bring back the food, and the lights, and the screens. It was going to give everyone in the world their own little kingdom." The old woman paused briefly to hitch up her trousers and scratch her earlobe.

Her granddaughter looked around at the sheep in the field. "So what happened?" she asked.

"Well," said her grandmother, rubbing her chin, tapping her pipe on the ground once again.

"No one really knows, not for certain, and this is just how I remember it, but there was this big ceremony a couple of weeks later, so I guess this toff thought she'd cracked it. Your great grandma took me and my sister to see it. Not too far from here, thinking about it." She gestured vaguely at some point in the distance. "This was back in the days when the city stretched all the way out here. Back before the land took it back."

The young girl stared at the horizon. "All the way out here?"

"Yeah. I remember when all this wasn't fields," said the old woman, wrapping herself up in her cloak. "So there was this massive crowd, must've been hundreds of thousands of us, so you can imagine the smell. But everyone wanted a look at the miracle." She leaned back slightly, drawing her knees up to her chest and folding her arms on top.

"So this toff woman walked out on to the stage, they wheeled out this big metal egg thing behind her, flashing lights all up and down the sides, and she starts talking, and talking about nothing, never quite getting to the point. You know, the way they do." The young girl nodded and shivered again. She thought she might just about be able to identify.

The old woman yawned. "So all this time, all you can hear around you is breathing. No one saying a word. Now, there's not nearly as many people around now, so I don't know if you can quite get your head around it, but for a hundred thousand people, that much quiet is a bit like noise in reverse. All you can hear is chests going up and down. And it was even stranger too, 'cos I was only nine at the time, and I'd never been in a crowd that big that wasn't throwing something.

"So eventually, the toff stops talking, and they wheel on this big red lever thing, and the breathing gets a bit louder now, 'cos you can hear they're hungry for it. And the toff says something I didn't quite catch, something about knees and strong arms, and a big jump for everyone, I don't know, they do talk a lot of shite, and she puts her hands on the lever. And now you can't hear anything at all. Not even breathing, which was even louder somehow."

The old woman smiled to herself and fished out her pouch again.

"So she pulls this lever, and the lights come on, and this big metal egg makes a whirring sound. And everybody breathes again. But not just that, 'cos there's shouting and cheering, and music for the first time in a long, long time."

She filled the pipe, lit it with another match and sat for a while, watching the sheep as a few of them stumbled about and lay down. "Looks like rain soon." She took a deep drag and hummed gently to herself. Her granddaughter sat patiently for a few minutes, then scowled and leaned forward.

"So then what happened?"

"Oh?"

"Well, what happened next?"

"Oh, right. Yeah." The old woman nodded. "So, we were all cheering and celebrating, and looking forward to the god-like power, and the egg's just sat there, thinking whatever thoughts something like that does. And suddenly, the people at the front, mostly the other toffs, start going quiet. Then the quiet starts to spread through the crowd."

"...What happened?" asked the young girl, tilting her head to the side, with narrow eyes. Her grandmother grinned, and the girl couldn't remember the lines on her face being so deep. Or her eyes so small.

"It turned itself off."

The young girl frowned. "...What?"

The old woman looked into the fire again, and her eyes turned bright yellow. "It turned itself off."

The young girl sat in silence for a moment, rubbing her neck, before looking back up at her grandmother. "Why?"

The old woman chuckled. "How should I know?"

"But didn't they turn it back on?"

"Of course they turned it back on. They built a brain out of tinfoil and wire. They weren't stupid."

"Well, what happened then?"

"It turned itself off again."

The young girl pursed her lips and looked down at the ground. "So, they turned it on. And it turned itself back off again."

Her grandmother nodded and let out a gentle plume of smoke, spiralling up to cut the moon in half. "Yep. Several times if I remember. They were still at it when we left."

The young girl sat and thought for a while, while the old woman emptied her pipe, until eventually she spoke. "That's sad."

Her grandmother chuckled again. "Is it? Or is it happy?" She stood up and kicked earth over the fire until the embers winked out. "I always get those two confused these days." She stretched and made a strange groaning noise, then pulled the young girl to her feet. "Anyway, the rain's on its way, so we'd best get you home. I'm already going to get it in the neck from your mum for letting you stay out this long."

They walked back in silence to little cabin on the other side of the hills, and that night the young girl dreamed of a metal egg on a hillside somewhere, sleeping under a blanket of rust. She hoped it had nice dreams.

Gabrielle Corry-Mead

Me and the minibar:
a letter of apology

To the staff of *The Grundy Hotel,*

T
HE CAB PICKED ME UP THE MORNING AFTER THE NIGHT BEFORE, when everything had happened. Judging by the bags under my eyes and the heftiness of my suitcase, the driver knew better than to ask if I was OK. Instead, he heaved the case into the boot and stubbed something into the satnav before setting off for the hotel. It was only round the corner, but for some Godforsaken reason a spark of dignity still burned away inside me, though it was rapidly disappearing.

Were I one of those insufferable sorts who gave complete dives marketable accolades, I would have described the Grundy as "vintage". As it is, I am not one of those people and saw it for the shithole it was. But it was cheap – or as TripAdvisor described it "an excellent overnight stop for the thrifty traveller" – so I booked a room.

"Do you have a lift at all?" I asked the receptionist, gesturing to my comically oversized suitcase. Julia had teased me from the day I bought it – "I'm not chucking you out just yet," she'd said.

The receptionist sighed and reached for the phone.

"I can call the porter," she said, "but he won't be here for another ten minutes."

I sighed.

"Don't worry about it, then. Sorry to have bothered you."

My key read "101", though there were not a hundred rooms by any stretch of the imagination and I read it as cruel joke by the hotel staff. Perhaps I am being unfair; miserable though the peeling brick wallpaper and Bates Motel shower curtain were, the room was clean enough and functional. I did not want a five-star suite with fluffy robes and chocolates on the pillow because then I would not have permission to mope – after all, who can mope with lobster on room service? – and what I really wanted right now was to sit in a cheap hotel room and devote one hundred percent of my being to unreservedly and unapologetically wallowing in self-pity.

For all the room's frugality, there was a small minibar at the foot of the bed. I did not drink back then – even now I limit myself to a glass of wine a week – but there was something strangely comforting in the knowledge that I could, theoretically, drink myself into a blissful week-long stupor on miniatures of Scotch that were better suited to the insides of a car than a human body.

"You'll go to pieces without me," she'd sneered as I crammed clothes into my case, "and you know what? It serves you right, you fat fucking whore."

"I'm not fat."

"Like I give a shit. Just get the fuck out of my fucking house."

"Jules…"

"Don't call me that."

"Fine. Julia, please; it's three in the morning."

"Then sleep on the fucking kerb for all I care, just get the fuck out."

(For those who are interested, I did sleep on the kerb.)

As I say, I did not drink and even if I did, I was all too aware of the extortionate prices that lurked inside hotel minibars. The week came and went, much to my indifference, and the solitary minibar and its contents remained untouched. It therefore came as a sickening surprise when I was phoned by the receptionist at the crack o' bloody dawn and billed for a week's worth of minibar drinks.

"But I haven't touched the damn thing," I stressed for the third or fourth time. "I don't even drink."

"Madam, we keep careful count of the beverages in each room and I can assure you…"

"There are fewer in my room than there were at the beginning of the week,. Yes, you've said, but I'm telling you I haven't touched them."

"Please, madam, you don't need to raise your voice."

"I'll do whatever I bloody well like until you start listening to me."

"Madam, please…"

I hung up. In hindsight I will agree this was a bad move and was not going to do me any favours. Much to my disappointment, the haranguing from the hotel did not end when I decided it ought to; week after week the bills kept coming and the threats of eviction became increasingly real. I was only allowed to stay because eventually I would have to cough up. I could have left as soon as that first bill had come through, but there was that spark again, refusing to admit defeat even when it was not only staring me in the face, but holding me at gunpoint on the edge of a cliff.

It will come as no surprise that I hated that minibar, the cause of all my misery. Every morning I would wake from a bad night's sleep to that tiny, yellowing fridge watching me. Every night I would turn out the light and the last thing I would see was that fading rectangular outline. There was no escaping it. I have later since discovered I was regularly heard screaming insults at the minibar, other times sobbing confessions to it.

Somewhere in the middle of all this I went to the police. I do not know what I was expecting, given that I had little to no evidence of my innocence, but all the same I went. A grey-haired sergeant shook my hand and offered me a seat. I explained myself as quickly and "sanely" as I could but he refused to believe me.

"It's not a question of what I believe, madam. There simply isn't the evidence to support your case. I suggest you pay the hotel and leave at the end of the week."

But I had not taken anything.

"Madam, we've been through this. There is nothing we can do until there is some evidence to give the hotel. Now, if you'll please…"

Isn't it your job to find evidence? You're the police, for Christ's sake.

"I would appreciate it if you didn't use that kind of language, madam. Now, I'm a very busy man and I do not have the time to detain you for abusing a police officer" Abusing a police officer? But I haven't done anything. Why was no one listening to me?

Minutes later, I found myself being escorted away from the station by a pair of police officers. I am still not sure exactly what I said or did to warrant my being thrown out but I did find a clump of hair in my hand when I returned to the hotel, and an oozing patch of blood on my scalp. Still the receptionist phoned for my bill, still the minibar remained. Of course it remained, it was a minibar. Why I was expecting it to have upped and left by the time I returned is beyond me, but still, there was something insidious about that lump of metal and plastic, and not just because it had "Fag lords must die" scratched on to its door.

"They're talking about us again," I said, putting my bag down beside Julia. "I'd give it a week before the letters start back up."

Julia shrugged and continued flicking absent-mindedly through the thousand and one television channels we owned but never watched.

"So what?'" she said, settling on some nature documentary or other. "Let them talk. It keeps them entertained."

"Great, so now we're the local freak show? Step right up, don't be shy; come and see our stomach-churning, blood-curdling rug-munchers in action!"

"There's no need to get like that."

I huffed.

"Fine. But when the hate mail comes shitting through the letterbox don't come crying to me."

"Why won't you leave me alone?" I wailed, hurling my rucksack at the offending appliance.

It toppled over with a satisfying thump, its door swinging open as it hit the ground. A couple of miniature gin and tonic cans rolled under the bed. I had to force myself not to pick them up. For a good long while I just sat and stared at the fallen little fridge and, even now, I believe it knew I was watching. The light faded and the overall greyness of the room deepened, the shadows contorting into monsters under the bed. Only the dim yellow light of the minibar kept the monsters from coming any closer and for the first time, I could not hate it. It was not its fault that I was living alone in a crumbling hotel, very nearly broke, with only an appliance for company.

The light had gone completely by the time it occurred to me I had never actually checked the contents of the minibar. Maybe there was nothing missing in the first place? Maybe the hotel was trying to extort a vulnerable guest? Should I phone one of those shows that exposes dodgy businesses? Would the pay out be good? With a little effort, I propped the minibar back up against the wall and began to inspect the interior. Given that I had not checked the contents at the beginning of my nightmare stay, I did not know what should be in there, but it did seem rather sparse. There were a couple of wine miniatures, one can of orange juice and three bottles of beer surrounded by acres of shelf space. I had not slept in several days and struggled to read the labels on the drinks; the world was becoming a strange whirl of yellow light, shadow monsters and illegible labels on fuzzy green backgrounds. Nothing was making any sense. I was not making sense. I thought I was going to see the infinite à la *2001: A Space Odyssey*, but a merciful thud plunged me into darkness and the infinite retreated back to whatever corner of space it lurks in.

Morning came with a dull ache to the back of the head and the discovery that I had slept head first in the minibar, I figured the door must have swung back and knocked me out. But the minor head injury and strange sleeping arrangement were by the by; it was what I saw when I woke that was of importance. At the very back of the minibar was a small gap in the bottom join. Figuring I must have missed this yesterday, I put one finger along the join. It was sticky and smelt like nightclub floors. A sharp edge against my finger caused me to recoil, and in doing so hit my head against the top of the minibar. Sucking the blood out of the small cut, I returned to the join to find a can of gin and tonic, crushed to paper-thin proportions. Someone must have been bored to do this. Carefully, I began dredging up more and more cans, crushed so finely it seemed impossible for a human to have done. I laid them out on the floor next to me and hefted over the minibar for one last inspection. On the bottom was a label, standard factory stuff, giving the details of the minibar and I would have given it no further thought had some very small print not caught my eye: "Not to be sold separately." In that moment, it all made sense, the missing alcohol, the crushed cans, the label.

"You're sad, aren't you?" I said, turning the minibar upright.

The minibar light blinked.

"I'm sad too, in case you hadn't noticed."

Two more blinks.

"I'm sorry I threw my rucksack at you."

A growling hum.

"I really am sorry, OK?"

The growl lowered to a quiet buzz. Neither of us should have been sold separately, but here we were, living alone in a crumbling hotel, one nearly broke, the other nearly broken, with only each other for company.

I therefore apologise wholeheartedly for the trouble I have caused you during my stay. Please find a contribution towards the beverages consumed.

Yours faithfully,

Room 101

PS You might want to use that contribution to purchase a new minibar or two as I have rehomed the room's previous occupant.

Helena Alice Cuthbert

Time and time again and again

Eyes of static impulse view the world through
a mind of white noise and pulsating thoughts.
Track the time, too fast, she's too fast, everyone else
is too slow with no exception. She takes the not real
voice of her reality but won't take the not real, real
people telling her no. She checks the time again. She infects
their too close, too loud bodies, radiation hits them hard
thuds them in the back, the force takes them,
they fall flat on their faces, surprise. She checks the time again.
No blame on her. Only on her head.
Medication poisons, dulls
her thoughts. No pain for them. They track her through the sessions
They say it's all OK. Truth in what they say is nothing new.
He tells her stop. She checks the time again.

Sam's parka

W HEN MY BIG BROTHER STILL LIVED WITH US, I used to have this
secret. It wasn't even that hard to keep, which was good because I
wasn't great at hiding things. I never really needed to be.

Sam, my brother, used to hang out with me a lot, but then he grew up
and learned to drive and he wasn't around so much any more.

"He's gone out," they'd say.

"Out where?"

"Jesus, just out! How am I supposed to know?"

Before Sam went out all the time we used to make forts while my
parents screamed at each other, and he'd make me practise arm wrestling so
I'd get tough. I always won.

It's not that our parents were divorcing. I'm pretty sure they loved each
other. I'm just really sure they loved their kids.

Sam left his cigarettes on his desk. There were about 4 empty packets
to every full one and even when they were all scrunched up, I still had to
check just in case there were any spare. I'd nick one really quickly, looking
around while I did it, then I'd nick his parka. It was bigger than me and
the sleeves stopped way after my arms did. You never had to remember a
lighter. He always had one in his pocket.

In the middle of nowhere you could walk down the road without
worrying a car might hit you. It was December and snowing and no one
was driving faster than 10 miles an hour anyway. I'd wait till I got to a big
empty field, where I were the only one who left footprints, and I'd watch
the smoke fill the air. It blew out in long streams, like magic, and I'd feel
for a little while like I was the only one that existed. I wanted to stay there
all night if I could, even in the cold. I hated coming home.

"Where did you go?"

"A walk."

"You smell like smoke."

"Yeah, I borrowed Sam's parka."

They'd nod and go back to watching the news or something. That was when they weren't fighting. When they were, they didn't notice me come in.

Sam went away to uni. My parents kept his room nice for him. I didn't realise how much I'd miss him when he went. And it wasn't just the cigarettes. By then I'd nick them off my friends or I'd stand outside shops asking strangers to buy them for me. I didn't like doing that though because sometimes they'd laugh at you instead of just saying no. I'd started to go out myself by then.

"Where are you going?"

"Out."

"Out where?"

"Just out! Fuck's sake."

It was always to more empty fields, or – even better – empty houses. I'd mix things up in two-litre bottles and have to hold it from the bottom when I drank. I'd wake up tasting vomit and have to walk around in the fresh air for a while before I could go home.

They still didn't know I smoked.

There weren't cigarettes on his desk when I needed one. That was when I found out Sam hid tobacco and king-size papers in-between the books on his bookshelf. I should've known. There was no other reason he'd have a copy of *Paradise Lost*.

The screaming had escalated to throwing plates this time. No matter how much you tried not to listen you could always hear.

"You're drunk again."

"Oh, yeah? And what are you then, dear?"

"I'm a good fucking parent at least. It's no wonder our son's failing uni."

"Oh, I'M the bad parent? If I remember correctly, you wanted our youngest aborted."

"Just me, was it? And who was it who found out too late?"

I didn't know why he hid the tobacco. My parents knew that he smoked. It were only when I rolled it out and found the plastic bag of weed that it made sense. I didn't want to get high, though. I just wanted a cigarette. So I'd roll them long with a king-sized paper, spent more time in the field lighting them then smoking them and they always seemed to fall apart. Still they were good, though. It was good to know they were there.

Sam didn't come home for Christmas this year. He's moved somewhere far away. My parents didn't mind because they're glad he's growing up. He doesn't smoke weed anymore, and he has a nice job with a nice girlfriend and managed to struggle through a boring degree. I miss him though.

It isn't often my dad gets violent but sometimes he snaps. On Christmas Day he broke a kitchen chair into kindling and fucked up all our posh plates. My mum was slurring her words. She said she was glad we were enjoying it since she got no help in the cooking. No help in anything for that matter. No wonder, she laughed, swinging her wine around, she had to get help elsewhere.

My dad banged his fist on the table and broke the glass. Some went in my mashed potato. I tried to sweep it off the plate but I cut my hand.

"Look what you've done, they're bleeding!"

"So!?"

I can buy cigarettes now if I want to. I look old enough. The problem is all the shops are shut on Christmas Day. Sam's room still has Bob Marley posters tacked on the wall and his ex-girlfriend's nudes under the mattress. I started pulling down the books from the shelf to find the secret tobacco so I could make a terrible roll. I took them all down and flipped through the pages but I couldn't find anything. He'd been gone a long time. He didn't take his parka, though, so I went for a walk. The problem was it weren't snowing like it used to, global warming and all, and it's just not the same without cigarettes.

When I woke up on the park bench on Boxing Day, I saw a few confused faces looking down at me and realised their voices probably woke me up. I walked for what felt like a long time, but it can't have been too far because I recognised the swings and the climbing frame.

"Are you OK?" one of them said. She looked old and kind and I sort of wished she hadn't found me. "Don't you think you might need to go home?"

I sat up and realised my hands were still wrapped in the pockets of Sam's parka. I played with the click on the lighter. Overnight it had started to snow. I was nearly home.

"Yeah," I said. "Maybe. But do any of you have cigarettes?"

Noah de Grunwald

Moon surgeries (i)

barefoot &
daggerhanded,
I stalk
your cottageside
at night,

sidling round back,
silent,
splay-toed,
crushing your geraniums
underheel –

the crickets sing
& the moon's a rosy
champagne wheel
swinging
from a dark country sky –

I come to
your kitchen window,
stop, and watch
you serve up shepherd's pie,
pootling back & forth inside –

in that orangey ovenly light,
your stovey stone walls &
dusky fireplace cracks;
kiddy-kids, widowed, & secrets
stashed in night cellars –

and my breaths make
a quiet mist on outside glass,
glazing;
& the deed sits
a big blunt weight within my fist

Static

and no one
ever stops and
wonders
where all these words came from:
these alien retches
on the flats
of our tongues, so
ancient and practised;
now sobbly-slobbled like
fast food –

and no one
ever stops and
listens to the strobe-lit hum
of the vending machine,
white &
wheezing
in the waiting room, in
the background
of a billion
shreds of bad news –

and no one
ever stops and breathes,
in –
out –

(shake it all about) –
don't cry.
breathe in the blue-masked
death of all things.
just learn to stop trying and
become the static.

Moon surgeries (ii)

the radio's on,
the pale baby's born,
& the minute-hand yawns

the hospital room,
the night window-view,
& pale snow melts the moon

the sleepers, their seats,
the dumb floor mopped clean,
& the vending machines

Gabriel Flynn

The hoover

THE THING WITH THE HOOVER WAS TYPICAL of the way Carl's stubbornness became such an issue. Carl had had that old Henry for years, since well before she moved in with him at the old house, and it was past its best. When they moved into the new house, Robyn thought it seemed like a sensible time to get a new hoover too, but somehow they ended up taking the old one with them.

The problem for Robyn wasn't an image or status thing – she's not one of these *Good Housekeeping* type women who needs to have a brand new, sexy vacuum cleaner on show for when her friends come around – the main problem was the smell; it had that very distinctive old-hoover smell, and it didn't just give off the smell when it was in use, it gave off the smell so powerfully that it would linger around the house for the whole rest of the day. Robyn didn't even like to wonder exactly what makes that old hoover smell.

The other thing was that the hoover hardly even worked any more. And so in the new house with the new sofas, and the dog and two cats who were all getting older and starting to moult, there was a real pet-hair problem. She couldn't get the pet hair up with the old hoover.

But Carl was an old-school socialist type, a trade unionist. He was in his fifties at this point, so he'd calmed down a lot, but still if they had to go anywhere at all upmarket or fancy (which they very rarely did), he would put on a very creased and crumpled shirt, so as to make at least a small statement of reluctance about going along with consumerist societal expectations and that kind of thing (often there would be a great deal of pet hair on the shirt also). He thought the hoover was fine. It did the job. It was past its best, he admitted, but as long as it still worked he didn't see the point in wasting money on a new one, not because they didn't have enough money (they did), but because this was exactly the kind of consumerist-society wastefulness that really got his goat, and would move him to do the thing where he would contort his face into an expression of incredulity and shake his head with a world-weary sigh (an affectation of his which really started to bother Robyn).

She would be doing the crossword and she'd start to think about it. She'd be getting so worked up that she wouldn't even be doing the crossword anymore, just looking at it while she thought about the pet hair, and the hoover, and the whole issue of his being very stubborn. Then she would resolve to take a few deep breaths to calm down so that her tone would suggest a degree of irritation and overall fed-upness much less severe than actually was the case, lay the newspaper down on her lap, turn to him and say, "Honey, let's just get a new vacuum cleaner."

At which he would do the incredulous head-shake thing and say, "Why bother? That one still works."

To which she would shake her own head, exhale, and say, "Fine."

This exchange would lead to what she would later refer to as The Hoover Impasse, where Carl would turn silent, retrieve the old Henry from under the stairs and start to hoover the whole house, always starting right there in the living room where they had been sitting prior to reaching The Hoover Impasse. He would hoover purposefully, in regular strokes but with varying degrees of aggression and conviction. It was a rhythm Robyn always thought was reminiscent of the way you'd beat a hostage tied to a chair. And during this prolonged, passive/aggressive hoovering, it would be very clear that he was conducting arguments with her in his head, and so she found it very difficult to sit in the same room as him while he did it, because it was as though she was in an argument in which she couldn't argue her side, but also because of the noise and the smell. So instead of sitting there and watching him hoover and argue with her in his head, wondering exactly what he was thinking about when he made an especially forceful motion with the hoover, shoving its nozzle hard into one corner of the sofa, she would take the dog out for a very brisk walk in the fields behind the house, and the whole time she would argue with him in her head about the hoover.

Usually when she got home from her brisk walk, he would have finished hoovering, but the house would be full of a kind of stillness like you imagine happens after a bomb goes off – the silence would seem not to be silence at all, just the absence of hoovering. The smell would be everywhere. The other thing was that he would always leave the hoover out for a while, rather than putting it back in the cupboard under the stairs, so that when she came through the front door, she would be hit by the eerie silence, the powerful and noxious smell, and the sight of the hoover just sitting there, even though Carl, at this stage, would be doing some job out in the garden that involved snapping branches or attacking an invasive weed.

When she told him she was leaving, he said, "Tell me why." And she told him a lot of things. It wasn't all about the hoover. There were other things too, of course. But she got to the hoover eventually.

After she left he didn't know what to do. In the evenings the cats and the dog would sit and watch while he drank strong ale and cried. Then, about three weeks later, he went and bought a brand new hoover: a Dyson Vax U90-MAR Air Reach Multicyclonic – all the reviews said it was the best on the market when it came to getting up pet hair. And it was quiet too. It was almost silent.

Alison Graham

Ten storey car park hymn

Oneiric,
whaling. Pool
of battery acid
and cellophane, swill
of diet pills. Small capsules,
a mouthful(l). The oesophagus
will survive harpoons, dynamite
even. We are talking formaldehyde

on a country lane. Knocks you right
out the water. And the atlas is a deadly thing,
the sound of it chortling and thumbing its way
into all we cannot hold. And us drooling at the lilac,
colour of waste light; committing joys and their serial
numbers to memory. Which we buy. Which we buy gladly.
Heart the size of a four-seater car. Ardently we eat the abdomen
out the sky humming all the way. I should be grieving the spacing of
my eyelashes and I am acned and hackneyed with a heart like a four-
seater, pickling. Pissing the megawatts away never looked so good as this.

Rebecca Graham

Toy soldiers

T HE FIRST TIME CORMAC SHOWED ME HIS GUN he wouldn't let me touch it. He pulled it out of a shoe box that he kept beneath his bed and held it up at me, like he would if he was going to shoot. He told me that his dad had had it for years.

I asked if it was loaded and he said no; his dad didn't use it any more so he'd stopped buying cartridges for it. His dad had a shop about two streets away in the town centre and he used to keep the gun there, in case there was a robbery. But he'd bought a new, better gun. So he didn't need this one anymore.

I asked if his dad knew that he had the gun. Cormac shrugged.

"He wouldn't care either way. It's empty, isn't it? It's like a toy."

That's when I tried to touch it. Cormac pulled it into himself, away from my hand.

"You're not responsible enough to hold it yet," he said.

For the rest of the day I watched Cormac pretend to shoot at various old toys in his room, passers-by in the street, and me.

A few days later I got a call from Cormac. I was playing this computer game from back in the 70s where you're a cowboy who has to shoot at Native Americans who run across the screen. I liked the little pixelated pools of blood that popped out of their heads when you shot them. It never mattered where you hit them; you could get them in the knee and their heads would still blow up. I'd just shot my sixth Indian when my mom came into the room with the phone held against her chest, saying I had a friend on the phone. She looked excited about it.

Cormac was breathless.

"I found some."

"Huh?"

"I found some cartridges."

"...for the gun?"

"No, for my fucking printer – yeah for the gun you fuckin' ass. Wanna go shoot some cans?"

I took my bike and met him at his house. He knew an isolated place about thirty minutes' cycle away, so we went there. We had to go along the main road for most of the journey, then turn off on to a dirt track which led through a bunch of trees for about five minutes. It opened up into a large, dried-out field which people evidently used as a sort of dump site. Cormac told me that someone else had told him that some guy was buried there.

We lined up a bunch of cans that Cormac had pulled out of the trash onto an upturned trough. Cormac had the first go.

He made the very first shot – hit the can right in the middle. We both jumped up and he started howling and beating his chest, gun still in hand. He grinned at me, holding his arms out.

"Dude, this shit is fucking easy."

It was a fluke.

For twenty minutes I watched him shoot and miss, shoot and miss, shoot and miss. I got up occasionally to pick up the odd ones that he hit, but mostly I just sat on an abandoned chair with my legs stretched out, waiting for my turn. He was getting frustrated; I could see the colour in his face darkening with every shot that he missed.

When he missed six cans in a row, he started to cry. He turned away from me and pulled his shirt over his head but I knew he was crying, I'd seen enough other kids do it to know what it looked like. He kicked furiously at a tyre on the ground and then took a short, circular walk that brought him back to his shooting spot.

"Fucking dust getting in my eyes," he mumbled, wiping his face with his shirt.

I didn't say anything. Cormac wasn't the sort of guy who would like someone pointing out that he was crying. A couple of years previously I'd seen him get into a fistfight with some other kid at school who had laughed at him crying after a detention. Cormac ruptured the guy's spleen. He was thirteen at the time.

He collected himself, grew still, and raised his arm. This time he shot four cans in a row.

We both got good pretty quickly. Cormac found a way to get more cartridges online and we both contributed to paying for them with money we stole from our parents.

We ploughed through our stock weekly. Cormac had a habit of shooting several rounds up into the air to celebrate hitting all his targets in a row. So he wasted a lot of bullets. He got a kick out of the noise and the drama, I think. I just liked hitting the target – that was all I focused on.

We shot at cans for another few weeks but eventually we started getting bored. One time, after hitting his target six times in a row, Cormac puffed air out through his mouth in a way that I guessed was to convey frustration and turned to me.

"They're just so *still*, y'know? Like, I can hit that now. But it's just sittin' there, so what use is it? People don't just sit there waiting for you to shoot them. They run about and shit."

He stopped and looked at me. I think he was waiting for me to question him, to find some fault in what he had just said but I didn't see why. He was right – people didn't just sit and wait for you to shoot them.

We tried shooting squirrels first. But they were too small and fast, and if you tried to shoot one then the rest of them would fly up all the trees and disappear.

"They're way smaller than people anyway," Cormac said, making circles in the dust with his toe. "We need something bigger."

"George."

"Huh?"

"Fucking George. My dog."

Cormac looked at me. I registered that his expression showed confusion. I thought he'd maybe misheard me, so I repeated myself.

"Fucking George. My dog."

He stared at me.

"You want to shoot your dog?"

I shrugged. "Yeah, why not? He's a pain in the ass. He barks in the night and he's old so he always dribbles everywhere. It's fucking disgusting, I hate him."

"How would you even do that?"

I shrug again. "Tell my parents I'm taking him for a walk and then say that he ran away or something, I don't know. Wouldn't be hard."

He carried on circling his foot in the dust, making the ring thicker and thicker. He didn't look at me.

"I dunno. It's your dog, man."

"Yeah. It's my dog."

We buried George at the edge of the field, about four feet deep. He didn't die as easy as either of us had expected. He kept whining and so we would shoot him again. He'd lie still for a bit and we'd think that that was it, but then he'd start crying again. So we'd shoot him. This happened four times and when I eventually decided to shoot him between the eyes to shut him up, Cormac was crying too.

This irritated me, but I didn't say anything. I just stared at the un-pixelated puddle of blood that was leaking out of George's mashed up head.

We sat next to the patch where we buried George and passed a bottle of whiskey that Cormac had stolen from his dad between us. We talked about who we would shoot if we could.

Cormac hated a lot of people. He hated that kid who had laughed at him when he was crying; he hated Sally Burgess for turning him down in the playground when they were fourteen; he hated Mr Davidson for making him look stupid in front of his class once; he hated Samuel Rudder, and his sister; he hated the entire football team; he hated the drama club too, for some reason.

When he had finished his list he asked me who I would shoot.

I didn't really know, because there wasn't really any one I hated. So I just shrugged.

"First person I see, I guess. Then whoever I see after that."

"That's pretty fucked up you know, man."

Then he started laughing. And I copied his laugh, because I didn't really know what was funny.

Lawrence Greenlee

Hunter among the stars

He lives in the moment.
More visceral than gemstones,
He doesn't shine like a king,
Like they said he should.
He swells every month
And hides secrets between his legs.

He is a man
Though his body falls in curves
Like unmapped hills
That he does not expect.
He craves cliff faces
And ocean strength.

He feels misaligned in horoscopes
And short-circuited.
His clothes don't fit
And his temper is an inch long.
He knows he's a constellation.
He just can't join the dots yet.

Faye Holder

Alphabet eggs

F AITH DIDN'T HAVE THE ANSWER. She stared at the others, her eyes pleading for someone, anyone to help her. Faith tapped out a staccato rhythm with her biro. No one noticed. She felt marooned on Table Island. The pen slipped from Faith's fingers on to the table, making a light tap. The gentleness of the sound was at odds with Faith's speedy thoughts. The moment to contribute her ideas had passed. She'd have to wait for another subject where she could offer up an obvious titbit. She was frustrated and annoyed and angry. Yes, that was it. She was angry. She decided she would channel her anger. She'd make it her bitch, but that phrase felt awkward in her head. She'd have to find something less manly, but that would involve reinventing the whole language, which she didn't have time for right now.

The question set in motion by the lecturer was rippling along the line of her seminar-mates, gaining strength and momentum, but her colleagues rode the wave with the effortless nonchalance of a surfer. Faith felt as if she was always being screwed over by language. Just once she wanted to get on top of it and ride it like the others did. But how could she be the fucker instead of the fuckee? How could she be the aggressor with her words when they were always fucking her? Her words seemed cumbersome and clumsy in comparison to her classmates. She had no words to speak with when it mattered, though they were there just under the surface.

As a young woman two places down from her answered the question, Faith thought about the language the islanders spoke. It was vaguely familiar, yet Table Island existed somewhere between reality and fiction. It felt pretty real to Faith: the buildings certainly felt like they were constructed from concrete; the rooms appeared to be square; the tables were definitely rectangular as Faith cupped their pointy edges in her hands. But the discussions people had in the square rooms were unlike any discussions she'd ever heard before, as they never seemed to relate to anything in the real world away from Table Island.

What the inhabitants of Table Island discussed seemed simultaneously to relate to everything else and nothing else Faith had ever experienced. Faith was used to objects being solid and reliable, but in this world, nothing was ever fixed. You'd put down your coffee only to come back later and find it had transformed itself into a carrot, or dog, or, worse still, an abstract thought. At least you could eat a carrot. The coffee now was not just a cup of coffee, but also a representation of "coffee" and all the things that coffee is, was, could be, should be, and never will be. Coffee could mean coffee beans, or the men and women that harvest them. These people could be Peruvian, or Rwandan, or Columbian. The coffee could be a sign of the workplace, of stressed-out office workers and secretaries, or of failing banks, the credit crunch, big bonuses and redundancies. The list was potentially endless. In her before life, no one had asked Faith difficult questions, because they hadn't expected anything of her. When Faith went to the coffee machine, it was just there in the same place it had always been, by the clocking-in machine. Faith was frustrated that nothing in this new world ever stayed fixed. Why could the coffee never just be coffee for once? It annoyed her that she could never get the letters to organise themselves right, or write, or rite, or wright. They never stayed still long enough. It was like on *Countdown* when she needed longer to make her paltry five-letter word. She'd be mystified at the bloke casually sipping water for the last twenty seconds before revealing his eight-letter word. An eight-letter word! Faith had solved the conundrum only once in her life: it was elephants. She had seen it right away. The words had never been that clear again. It was as if Carol Vorderman had ascended a cloudy mountaintop with the *Countdown* clock strapped to her back while Faith peered at the clock through binoculars from a moving bicycle, only the bicycle was now a unicycle, and Carol Vorderman was now Rachel Riley, and she was holding a steaming cup of coffee, or was it 'coffee'? Faith had given up trying to decipher the difference. She was also starting to question whether it really mattered, perhaps coffee could be anything you wanted it to be.

The question had moved on to the next person along the table. Faith watched as the Table Islander leaned forward in his chair; he was settling in. He was going to be a while; this was Faith's opportunity really to pay attention to the words coming out of his mouth. Faith grasped the first few sentences. He was saying something about gender and language, and then her mind drifted away again like the ebbing tide. Table Island was just one in a long chain of islands in the alphabet archipelago, castaway in a vast ocean of thoughts.

At the same time every year on Table Island, complete sentences would tumble on to shore; their backs thick with punctuation barnacles as they heaved their clumsy literary bodies up the beach and buried their alphabet of eggs in the sand. The birthing was so exhausting that many of the complex sentences would die in the process, leaving their little eggs to fend for themselves. Weeks later, the solitary letters would heave their way up through the sand and race along the beach, the wind blowing about their serifs majestically. But before they could reach the sea, they would have to run the gauntlet of poets lined up by the surf, pens and papers poised in their grubby hands, eager to wrestle the defenceless little newborns into their poems. But if the letters survived the trauma of the word wranglers, they were free to explore the ocean of thoughts for themselves. Some letters quickly worked out that there was safety in numbers, or rather words, but others struck out alone – these were called the alphas, but they were extremely rare, and some even questioned whether the fabled "A" and "I" words existed at all.

While Faith was preoccupied with alphabet eggs, the conversation drifted away even further. She studied the unspoken language the man who was sat next to her was projecting into the room. Somehow he made himself wider than anyone else, though he was no bigger than any of the other men in the room. He leaned back in his chair, paused, thought for a bit before jiggling his foot as he spoke. Faith could feel the vibrations in her toes and the balls of her feet. No one interrupted him, everyone seemed to just know that this was a pause to be respected, even admired. Everyone waited for him to organise his thoughts and then articulately express them like he was drizzling honey over his porridge. Faith's fingers tapped out a distress call on the underside of the desk. She needed the words in her head to stop meandering about like they were on a Sunday stroll. They needed to organise themselves into neat sentences so she could answer the question that was lapping at her feet.

No one could hear her pathetic cry for help now. Faith's fingers pressed into something squishy on the underside of the table. Gum. What could it mean? She pondered its stickiness for a moment, before concluding that the reason it was sticky was because it had been in someone's gob.

Why couldn't it be that simple? The fact that it was attached to the table, the object that symbolised her remoteness, got lost somewhere on the superhighway that carried her thoughts around her brain. All Faith could think was: bastard! Who puts gum under a table at university? She always had trouble distinguishing the important points.

Faith had done it again. She'd really tried to concentrate that time, but then she'd felt the gum and it sent her off on the tangent about sticky things not making sense. Now she was thinking of Post-it notes. Shit! What was her neighbour saying? Faith tuned in again. The man was now talking about some women being sexually aroused while riding horses. She wondered how this part of the conversation came about and why no one else found it funny.

Faith looked up and saw a spider in the corner of the room, hovering above the islanders like a miniature deity, spinning webs made out of tiny Ts and Hs. She nicknamed the spider Maureen. She suspected Maureen had a better grasp of the conversation than she did, only she couldn't express it because there was no discourse for spiders to communicate. But Faith suspected that if Maureen could express her thoughts, she'd probably be much more articulated than her. Screw Maureen! Who cared what spiders had to say anyway?

The room had gone quiet. The Table Islanders were all looking at her. Faith stuttered out a few random words. She could feel her face turning red and her frustration growing as she tried to structure her thoughts. She felt as if they were butterflies escaping through an atrium window. The windows were too high for her to reach up and close. She'd run outside to try and wrangle them back in, but the wind would buffet them further and further away from her, until they were like full stops on blue paper. The trouble was Faith didn't have a big enough net, but then she suspected there wasn't a net big enough in the entire world that was capable of capturing all her thoughts. Faith's words petered out and the chatty man next to her picked up the discussion again. Faith sat quietly and let him do the talking.

As her classmates filed out of the classroom, Faith noticed something wedged in Maureen's spider web. She walked across the now empty room to get a better look. The web was not just made up of letters, as she thought earlier, but there were words in it now too. And not just random words, but the words she lost during the seminar.

ideas

     no   words   letters

     Words

     superhighway   language

         thoughts

concentrate

     thoughts

                   reach

further   important   always

            from

   have

then   big   talking

           world

capturing

                         Faith

The words that fell from her head were all here in Maureen's web, caught together in no particular order. From Faith's removed vantage point the words looked marooned like tiny islands when seen from a plane high above, sometimes the clouds would clear enough to see the whole chain of them, but most of the time they were hidden by thick clouds.

Jules Ignacio

extract from *Lover, exist*

a cheek-slap – Sir Midas – !
    & my skin turns into gold,   as beautiful as a smear, bulging –
a heartbeat only certain lovers can
conjure. nighttime, live & drunk,   when the moon
drips. arms pinned, pulled free, pulled the filaments,
                    kissed the neck as passionate as breaking clavicles.
his hair the sea, & I can only drown. in honey dusk, death is the only other
   poet, so give in!
no future, no past. give the figure a name! the limbo
      still does not chant! give the utterance its deserved physicality! Sir
   Bliss. ask for encore as a verb, redefine
another cliff to freefall from, hit-hard, shattered-shuddering, like a flicker
   in a cacophony,
away from my own storms, my seasons unfit for mourning skies,
      & it is only Sir's rhetoric, Sir's rhetoric that harms and mends.
   Sir Balladeer heeds, & i tug Clotho's white robes. Sir Balladeer heeds,
   & i clip Clotho's fingers to keep her from spindling! Sir Balladeer heeds,
   & i create & announce, clip a bell on myself, the malignant churchspire.
the malignant present tense that i try to eat, then churn, then vomit as
   worm-meat as
gleaming as a fat jewel hanging from greed's tongue.
              i may be mistaking illusions for love.
i may be looking for love   in those places humming darkness.

#chemsex

under the dim kinklight, we throw our shadows down. no path to walk,
   no space,
only craving, no pause.   in brutalism, we are abandon. thirst   in slit
hearts & indelible moans. brain-dead,   nose-numbed, blind &   dumb.
be   men & i the ghost. say i've got a steely stare. kiss   me
badly to guillotine my tongue & leave it in the floor like a dusted heart,
all wriggling & bubbling blood.   sex is a race & stimulants the course.
coke-sprinkled cocks.   a lad with gnarled hands
pumps more meth into me, &   i take a puff   to   ease the
palpitations.   i pant & shudder, while being   sucked.
next to me, a guy guzzles   another's piss, &   the
pissing   looks at me straight in the eyes
after catching my stare, then smirks. i philosophise.
heidegger says,   'every man   is born as many
men and dies a single one.'   men collect in the dirt   like ants
on sweet things.   a   thinking body   can only hope.
i love everyone.   i want everything.   i kneel & drink.

I speak of rust

Body into lead, rock-hard heart
    that shook,
    then fell with electric violence.
Killing myself
    like you is an art form I've always
struggled to master—
you not a photograph emblazoned
by one instant, you not a beat
before the percussions.
Masqueraded those beliefs by the gutters,
    drunk-dancing
into sunrise – those sweet
features belying romance. Submerging,
I still ask myself why. You have   never
filled the shoes, never shook
    lightning out of cloud-mouths
        through which moths
speak in fabric stains.   Dirt has been
contained out of time, clinging on
walls that speak rust.

I've always wanted
to embody the suffering in your scars.

The fool that aligns passion with life used
to create genius in the form

of metamorphosis.
 Everyone, you told me,
    has killed you.
        You knew that.
You never realised how much I love you.

Marked

C EMETERY WAS SILENT. Drops of rain began trickling down. Justin trudged along, boots branding the mud. Few moments later the rain was pouring down, water slowly drowning his footprints, attempting to erase his marks. It'd succeeded in covering them up, but the cloak was transparent. They remained. A half-faded reminder.

He halted before Vincent's tombstone. Funeral had been a drowsy chore, as expected. No one'd shown up. Even the revered Father barely deigned to babble a few words before scurrying off into the church. Mattered little, anyway. Justin had a feeling that his sermons of forgiveness and redemption weren't ever going to settle in Vincent's stubborn skull. 'Specially not now.

"Gloomy place they put you in, Vinnie," Justin said.

The leaves on top of the grave were sinking into the dirt.

"Yeah, yeah, don't laugh too much. Standing in the rain, right in the bloody bog for you."

The wind rushed past the grave's surface, dragging the leaves along with it.

"Never were that talkative, were you?"

Leaves were rustling. Branches waving in the wind.

"I'll try not to be too long, yeah?"

Justin turned around and started walking back towards the exit.

He stopped, looked back. A silhouette standing next to Vincent's grave. A man, staring down at it. Tall, even taller than Vincent. Lanky. Wasn't moving, or shielding himself from the rain.

Justin squinted at him. A negro.

The man's head turned. Gazing back. His face a mask: rigid, unflinching. Justin waved at him. The man tilted his head to the right. A few moments passed. He didn't move. Justin turned around. Could still feel his stare crawling on him as he walked through the entrance.

Been travelling across the Atlantic for weeks. Thunder and uneasy waves roiled outside. Constant rattle. Waves clawing at the shutters. Justin would have minded, but at least the racket drowned the moans and cries from below deck.

Vincent spent most of his hours down there, whip in hand. Passed the time with it, he said. When he was feeling creative, he'd go for the iron. No more than a plaything for him.

A knock on the cabin door. It screeched open.

Vincent entered.

"Justin."

"Vinnie."

He grabbed a chair and dragged it across the floor. Put it down next to Justin and sat down.

"Got us some work to do, Justin," he said.

Little had changed since Justin's last visit. Churchyard still greeted him with the familiar gloom. Still boggy. Mushy. Boots caked in no time.

He walked up to the tombstone.

"Apologies for being late," he said. "Know I said I'd try, but – four years go by quicker than you'd think. Dunno if it's the same for you at... wherever they decided put you." He sighed, gaze wandering. "You know, I been thinking, Vinnie, about –"

He was there again. Staring at Justin. As if he'd never stopped. This time Justin didn't wave. Took a step forward. The man began walking towards him. His back was hunched.

"Good evening," he said. He was gaunt, thin skin stretched over his cheekbones.

"Yeah, evening," Justin said. His hand offered itself, and then Justin pulled it back. Scratched his head with it.

"I think I have seen you before," the man said. African accent was screaming through his words. Songhai. The south-west.

"Well, I know I've seen you before. Four years ago. Standing next to this grave here." Justin tilted his head at Vincent's grave.

"Yes, I remember that as well," he said. "You were looking at me. And then you waved."

"Didn't return the favour," Justin said. "Call a man curious for wondering why a stranger's standing next to his friend's grave."

The man laughed. "Yes, I understand. I merely like to walk around here when I visit."

"Visit?"

"My son," the man said. He pointed at the back of a tombstone behind him. "This day, every year."

"Oh," Justin said.

He was about to turn around.

"He was only four years old, sadly. Starvation."

Justin stood still. Nodded. "Tragedy, that. Sorry."

The man shook his head. "A lifetime ago."

"No, still," Justin said. "Should never happen."

"But unfortunately it did," he said. "And unfortunately I must go. My wife is waiting for me. She can get a little impatient." He laughed again.

"'Course, yeah. Sorry to have kept you."

The man waved at him as he walked away.

Headed down the stairway. Vincent opened the door.

They were all squeezed into their quarters, leg-irons rooting them in place. Most crouching, legs trembling and wobbly. Some fallen to their knees, scraping wood as the ship shook. Choice between life in your legs slowly fainting or your knees' skin slowly peeling off.

Sweat began trickling down Justin's face. Air was thick and putrid, the kind that clogs your nostrils. Kind you don't want to be breathing. Slaves were coughing, floor oozing with mucus and phlegm. A child lay in their midst, nameless. Some were staring at Justin as he passed them by.

Vincent was tall enough to have to hunch as he walked along. He shoved them aside and eventually halted next to a male slave.

"This one here," he said.

Justin nodded.

"You know why I brought you down here, Justin," Vincent said.

"You know how to do this yourself," I said.

"Mm-hmm. And you don't." He offered Justin the iron.

Justin stood before the tombstone again. He noticed some cracks.

"Evening, Vinnie," he said. "Not half bad this time, yeah? Two years. Not bad as four; gimme that much."

The tombstone the man had pointed to as his son's still lay there amidst the others.

"Strange days, Vinnie. Not easy without you looming over my shoulder. No secret I always wished for you to leave me in peace, yeah? Guess I wasn't being careful enough with that." Hands in his pockets. "Started having some nightmares, too. Never got those when you were around."

"Good evening, Justin." Justin turned around. The man had appeared again.

"Evening –" Justin cleared his throat. "Sorry, you never – I mean, might have forgot your name."

"Not to worry, my friend. You never asked for it."

"Right."

"My name is Babatunde."

"Babatunde. Good to know."

The man raised a brow. "You pronounce it very well."

"Yes, I've been to – been to Africa a few times, yeah."

"You have? How so?"

"I was – just some expeditions," Justin stammered. "You know, exploration. Treasure-hunting. That sort of smart endeavour."

The man laughed, yellow teeth peeking below his top lip.

Justin gave way to a chuckle.

"Still visiting your son there?" he asked.

"Yes, of course. I've never forgotten."

"Don't expect you to," Justin said.

The man was smiling. "I'm glad that you remembered," he said.

"'Course."

The man started nodding, eyes crawling up and down again.

Justin tore his stare away from him. "So, uh…"

"It was good to see you again, Justin."

"Yeah, pleasure."

He walked by his son's grave as he left. Not one glance.

Justin had the iron. Scorching heat from its crimson surface. Close enough to cook his cheek. He turned it away from his face, towards the man's back. Bones eager to break through thin veil of his skin. Barely anything on him for the branding. Vincent grabbed a part of the upper back, below the neck. Slapped it once, looking at Justin.

Justin held on to the man's shoulder. Brought the iron down. It hissed on impact, steam coiling. The man's attempts at screams were pathetic; a low whining sound carrying him through it. Didn't struggle. Barely shook. Justin could feel the symbols pressing into him, leaving their mark.

He lifted the iron. Charred flesh moulded into letters. Black bits. Vincent let go of the man and he fell forward.

"Give that here," Vincent said. He took the iron away from Justin.

Vincent's name on the tombstone had started to fade. Letters were growing pale, absorbed into the stone.

"Late again," Justin said. "Sorry about that. Probably getting a bit bored down there. Doubt they're giving you the whip to pass the time."

He was shivering, rubbing palms together.

"Yeah, can't help but doubt you're anywhere but down there," Justin said. "Didn't bother you, did it? Never bothered you."

Wind was howling, harsh and cold.

"Least it never caught up with you, Vince. Always got a good night's sleep. Sure of it. Never had to wrap your head 'round anything."

Justin turned around. For the first time he saw the man standing next to his son's grave. Still not looking.

He found himself walking up to him.

"Cold day," Justin said.

"Oh, yes," the man said. "But I think you would agree that it is preferable to the heat."

"Tough choice you're giving me."

"Yes, perhaps. You have to experience both, I think, to make the choice."

The man's gaze fell on Vincent's tombstone.

"I see you continue to have quite spirited discussions with your friend."

"We do," Justin said. "Little more one-sided than they used to be."

"But you still talk. Even without his answer."

"Bit easier to talk to him now, honestly."

"Truly?"

"Yeah, truly."

The man stood silent for a while. "I have to say, I am quite surprised."

"Really?"

"You still visit him, you still talk to him."

Justin shrugged.

"I have to assume you did not always get along that well?"

"Not all the time maybe, no." Justin glanced at the tombstone. "Seems I get along better with the dead."

The man nodded.

"Right," Justin said. "Might go somewhere a bit warmer after all. Not too keen on freezing."

"Of course."

Waters had calmed. Waves now decided to whoosh along, a fitting companion to the mute night. Justin stood on the edge of the deck. Away from the pile.

They were getting close to the port. Bristol was only a few days away and they would finally get rid of this batch. Sell it, go back for the next one. Meant at least a few days of quiet.

The splash was sudden and loud. Ripples spread around the body. Would float on for some time before it sank. Vincent had already lifted another, approaching the edge.

"Pretty night and everything," he said. "But you can still enjoy it while helping me dump these ones."

"Loses a bit of its charm that way, don't you think?" Justin said.

"Trust me, the smell will make it lose all of its charm." He flung another overboard.

Justin walked over to the corpses. Grabbed one by the armpits, dragging it over the floor. Planks were creaking. Thin and emaciated as it was, he still struggled to lift it over the side. Eventually it tumbled downwards.

Vincent was staring at him.

"What?" Justin said. "It's heavy."

Silent.

Justin sighed. "What is it? Don't want me dragging them?"

Justin shook his head, moving over to the pile. Vincent wrapped one arm around him, grabbing his shoulder.

"Leave it, I'll do the rest," Vincent said.

"You serious?"

"Dead serious."

He gave Justin's shoulder a final jolt and walked up to the pile. Justin went back to watching the waves.

The quiet in the cemetery was gone. First time Justin noticed any of the sounds coming from the harbour. Ships docking and departing. Bell echoing through. Even the susurrus of bellows, yells, and cries all entangled into one.

Vincent's gravestone was standing where it always was.

Justin's eye caught on to the son's tombstone. He walked up to it.

Its front identical to the back. No name on it. Traces of weeds peeking out through its thin cracks, yet no trace of any letters on its surface. It remained nameless. No more than a piece of rock plunging out of the dirt.

Francesca Kritikos

canned peaches

our love is a fairy-
tale: if you won't rescue me,
i won't fuck you. i am weary
in this trailer park – we
don't have castles in
America. i can't feel like a queen
eating Costco canned peaches. sin
is all i have left, but i'm unseen:
that's what we call innocence here.
lift my silk dress, ignore my abscesses –
at our motel-honeymoon, what will you wear?
husband, King, all i crave are excesses.
one day, i'll get out of this place, i know.
i first said that fifteen years ago.

the witch's house

her canopied house, the one the trees
bent over as if hiding her shame,
burned down last year. we were there.
we smelled the smoke in the air,
heard the sirens. we had all done our time
peeking through the mouse-chewed holes
in her garage door, flattening her fat
plants to sniff the concoctions of her
garden, as if we could taste her poison
on our child-pink tongues. we had
never seen her, but we knew the things
only children can know,
the way witches make vibrations
in still summer air. we felt them through
the hot asphalt where we loved & hurt
each other. she made her way into us –
witches are always impostors, too.
our thick & plump hearts stung
as we ran past her house like
victims & thieves, like everything.
her house burned down. we were there.
now the trees are gone: her shame melted
with her & the rubble is her punishment.
dead or alive, we don't know.
we never saw her, but we felt her bites,
we felt her knock out our milk teeth.
they are gone now, like the trees.

les dieux

the gods are eating grapes
i haven't understood them
for the past two winters
my mouth is a frozen door
that eats when it can
and starves, and starves
if i worked my fingers raw
i'd never make the things
that they can make
kneeling is understanding
but it's hard to kneel
in all this blood, my blood

milk carton kid

i hold soap in my mouth
to freshen impure words
and when i sleep like an angel
i dream of hell.
we are living in a house
painted white but streaked
with blood. in a hidden box
you keep small parts of me.
i find them and let you have them.
our lives are a movie,
hazy and freckled with voids.
i don't look too close.
i am walking home from school.
a man in a car won't let me go.
the sky is sunny like a burst celestial flower,
fractures lining its petals.
i imagine walking through the woods
where streets get cut off until they resurface
with the crookedness of a missing child's
forest preserve bones.
i am that child
and i am at home.

Patrick Lally

Approaching poetry

P presses that circular depression – with its little square centre – a hundred
times an hour, but **S.**
Jobs' fridge is bare.
Q has, through longing, stretched his usual unit:
Chronometric Malform

P & **Q** opt for a fruity film – @ £7 a ticket – with a runtime promising
eighty-eight *min.* Thirty pass
she whispers.
P rights his gaze (smiling) and finds credits (rolling):
Temporal Collapse

P has no words left for **UEA** but multiple hundred for **Q** – through **Z-Berg**
– crafted with care + some love premature.
ü Seen 22:11   yet returned half-sized
                in twice the time:
Inter-Network Cleft?
                Drag?

P drinks beer and **Q**, a heady cocktail.
She leaves him / with a dozen empties / without inebriation:
So{m}br{e}iety

A ¹/₂ gram of potassium, 3450 calories, and 94*mg* of caffeine sees **P** (squinting)
through a 14-hour
day.
But minding **Q**'s lash-long blink has him (*sans*-stimulant) going 24:
Amorous Sustenance

He arrives at **Q** Underground, in a Northerly line; though sunken in this
subterrane, he floats.
On departure, air-bound, **P** sinks as Gatwick shrinks:
Gravitational inversion

P is placed alpine; up a peak, in a chair, he faces views arresting and
inimitable.
In a mountain tip dipped pink he marks her mouth:
Cerebral compulsion

Q tempers hot to cold (when between them an expanse spans)
giving **P** chill blains.
Though he knows – despite his face – he pursues the pain:
Intuitional Regression

Q is without clothing & beyond compare, but has some bad news
regarding regularity.
She softens with a blow, still **P** is belittled:
Libidinal Defection

P approaches **Q**, says *[he's] tried [his] hand at poetry...*
Q skims through, *thoughts are wont to amplify feelings*, and renders him
mute.
**Merely the behaviour of a vast assembly of nerve cells (and their
associated molecules) evoking**
psychosomatic pangs of a socially-constructed, metaphorical, nature:
"Heartache"

Coffee stains

I SIT ON THE FLOOR. IT'S NOT MY FLOOR. IT'S FELIX'S FLOOR. Here he comes now, sleep-stained, hair a knotted mop on his head. He flicks through a pile of envelopes and mumbles something about the rent. It's his rented floor. Rented flat – or apartment, as they say here. It's draughty and patchy and has a smell like wood. This room is half swallowed by the grand piano. I sit underneath it.

Felix carefully lays the envelopes on the coffee table. "Morning, Erica," he says.

"Hi."

He looks at me, amusement colouring his face, as if I'd said something funny. He says, "Breakfast?"

I say, "Yes."

He stands under the archway between the living room and poky kitchen. He folds his arms, leans against the wall, eyebrow raised. Just looks at me. Then he nods, smiles, and pours Coco Pops into two bowls. We sit down at the little white table in the kitchen. It's dabbled with tea spills. "Needs cleaning," I say.

Felix looks up from his cereal. "What does?"

"The table," I say.

"Oh." He wipes it with his sleeve. "After breakfast."

I look out the window at the dark brown clouds spilled over the sky. The glass smudges everything. "Windows need cleaning," I say.

"It's just the glass. It's like that."

"Oh." I look at my spoon. Suddenly I feel it needs cleaning, too. My eyes drift to the window again. Manhattan's skyline is out of sight, lost somewhere under the coffee-stained sky.

"My stuff's clean, you know," Felix says, his eyes locked on the spoon that I'm rubbing with my sleeve. Concern is so visibly etched on his face that I stop.

"Is something wrong?" he says.

I sit on my hands to stop them cleaning the spoon again. "Why would something be wrong?"

"You seem tense," he says. "And you're frowning."

"No, I'm not."

"Yes, you are. Your eyebrows are all screwed up."

I look outside again. Before I came here, I imagined what the view from the flat might look like: the Brooklyn Bridge all lit up at night, the city lights sprinkled along the river like gold dust. It's not quite that, but somehow there's a curious charm in the brick-faced Bushwick apartment block, with its fire escapes scrawled all down the walls.

"Erica?"

My hands are sticky. "I'm going to the bathroom," I say.

I don't like how the towel feels. It's scratchy and damp from other people's hands. I rinse mine again. Then Felix knocks on the door.

"Erica? Can I come in?"

"Mm." I turn the tap off.

He walks in, smiling, stands there with the door open. "I'm taking the day off," he says.

"What?" I say. "Why?"

"Well, I figured it wasn't fair for you to spend another day by yourself. You're still so new to the city. I thought I'd show you around." And he just stands there smiling, eyes shining and hopeful.

"Uh…" You can't do that, I want to say. You can't afford to take days off work. I'm not that important. But I don't say this. I don't know why.

Instead Felix adds: "Why were you sitting under the piano earlier?"

I shrug. "I always sit under the piano."

"I know," he says. "I found you asleep there the other day. You'd taken all your blankets with you."

I twist my hands, feeling sort of self-conscious that he'd seen that. "I don't know. I like it there."

Felix nods. "That's cool. I just thought there was something wrong with the sofa."

"There is," I say, sort of smirking. "It needs cleaning."

We take a cab into Manhattan. Even when we reach Central Park, it's early; through the cracks in the clouds, the sun is still dripping its pale early morning colour. Winter mist clings to the grass and curls round my feet. And all round, behind the scrawny leafless trees, the buildings stand in perfect squares.

"I wish we were in a helicopter," I say.

Felix walks beside me, hands in his pockets. "So do I," he says, absently. His face is turned to the sky, smiling, eyes lost behind the veil of a daydream. Then they narrow in confusion. "Wait, why?"

"Because from above," I say, "we could see how perfect it is. The park is a perfect rectangle."

"Ah, of course," he says. A gush of wind suddenly rushes at us, and his scarf flies behind him. It hits him in the face, and I realise I'm laughing. Felix laughs too, his eyes bright. And our walking slows till we're still.

"Do you know what I think is perfect?" he says.

We stand beneath a tree. The sunlight slips through the branches and dapples the ground. I twist my hands, not really sure how to stand still.

"What?" I say.

He narrows his eyes, as if in concentration, his gaze fixed on mine.

He says, almost whispering:

"The Skylark by Balakirev."

I blink. "What?"

"The Skylark by Balakirev. It's an arrangement of part of an opera by Glinka. Farewell to Saint Petersburg, to be exact."

"Oh."

"It starts with a beautiful alto melody, although in the opera it's usually sung by a tenor, and then it flows into little tinkling high notes. The alto notes are the person, and the high notes are the bird. The song illustrates the man talking to the bird, and the bird answering."

"But birds can't – "

"The first section sounds delicate and soft and cautious. And then the alto melody is played again, but more virtuosically, and the music sort of fills up."

Felix's whole face lights up, and I know he'll start talking in the way he does when he's excited, when his voice grows animated and his words seem to fall out of his mouth in strings.

"It becomes richer, but still hushed. Then there's a part where the music trills, fluttering, like a butterfly dancing across the keys."

"But butterflies aren't heavy enough to – "

"And this is the genius part." His hands dance about like his imaginary butterfly. "The rest of the piece is a kind of variation on the two previous melodies. They interweave, like layers. Like they were so beautiful that they fell in love and had a baby, and that baby is the new melody. And then the music trills and dances again, faster than I could ever play, and it's perfect."

He smiles, eyes sparkling. The cold white sunlight falls softly on his face. I start to laugh.

He scrunches his eyebrows, confused. "What's so funny?" he says.

"I don't know," I say. "You. The way you talk. All over-excited like that."

"Oh." He smiles at his feet. "You know, you talk like that sometimes, too."

"Do I?" I say. "When?"

"Well, you used to a lot. When you would talk about New York, and how you'd live here one day. You knew everything about the city, more than I do now, even when you'd never been."

I feel unsettled remembering this. Because New York was safer from far away. It was numbers and pictures and shapes on a map. Real New York is a different place, a physical, breathing, concrete thing, made of noise.

Now the misty sunlight explodes in one corner of the city, and from there the sky unrolls, bruised and bursting. Skyscrapers poke into the clouds, and seeing that skyline now, something catches in my chest. The realisation that I'm here, that this is where I live, settles quietly and irrevocably in my mind.

"Aren't dogs supposed to be on the leash here?" Felix says, noticing a dog stuff its nose into a paper bag. I hear the bag crinkling. I hear the dog's scuffing breath. Something twists uncomfortably in my stomach. Everything around me has grown larger and louder, and all I can think is that the whole world needs to fold itself up into a tiny piece of paper that I can stuff inside a box and hide somewhere.

I feel Felix's mood shift with my own. "Hey, are you OK?" he says.

"I…" I can't talk anymore. Too much air is swelling inside my head. The noise of my jacket rubbing against itself every time I move crawls into my brain, contorted and amplified. I try to yank myself free of it, tearing at the zip, but it's stuck, my hands are shaking, it's too small, I can't grab hold of it.

"Erica?" Felix says. "Is everything OH? You're shaking." He comes closer and rests his hand on my arm and I flinch and fall backwards and scramble to the foot of the tree. The sun's gone. My shoes are muddy. I squeeze my eyes shut.

He sits beneath a tree a few feet away, shadows and sunlight sliding across his face. The air in my head clears, and everything grows softer, slowly.

"Felix…"

He looks up and comes over, sits beside me. It's one of those bright, sharply cold days, and the wind coils round my fingers. There are no words in my head, so we're quiet for a while, till Felix says:

"Did something happen? That made you feel like that?"

I shrug, thinking about this huge, sprawling, tripping city, with its buzzing, thumping lights and sounds and people and cars and cabs. I try to explain. "It's just…"

The words dissolve. A lilting birdsong sails down from above us, and we look up at the branches that cradle us in their shadow. I say, "You know, virtuosically isn't a word."

His eyes fall to meet mine. "What?"

"When you were talking about the Skylark," I say. "You used the word virtuosically, but it's not a word."

"Oh." His face lights up in a smile again. "Well, it should be."

I move to sit closer to him.

"One day," he says, "we're going to have an apartment on the Upper East Side, overlooking the park."

"And we'll be able to see how perfectly perpendicular all the buildings are," I say. *We're going to*, I think.

The day ebbs away, and outside the cab window, the sky's dressed in pink. Beethoven's face hangs on a purple flag above a shop.

"This is 58ᵗʰ Street," I say. "Piano row."

Felix looks at me in surprise. He grins. "That's right."

The taxi's reflection ripples in the storefront windows we drive past. I say, "Did you know the first taxi company in New York was introduced in 1897? It was called the Samuel's Electric Carriage and Wagon Company, and they ran electric hansom cabs."

I hear the driver chuckle. Felix laughs too, and I watch out the window as the city spills by, the streets unfolding like a map.

In the musky, wooden smell of the living room, I trace circles on the table with my finger. I'm on the sofa. Felix calls from the kitchen: "Coffee?"

"No thanks."

"Suit yourself."

He comes in soon after, cup in hand, laptop cradled under his arm. He crawls under the piano with them. Then he grabs a piano book and spreads it out on the floor.

"What are you doing?" I say.

"I want to show you something," he says.

Confused, I clamber under the piano after him. On the screen is a YouTube video of the Skylark.

"Listen to this," he says, "and you'll see how perfect it is."

He presses play. The music flows out and he traces the notes that scrawl across the paper like fire escapes.

"Why can't you play it?" I ask.

"Because I can't play it," he says. "Not well, at least. Now, ssh. Listen."

Then as he goes to turn the page, he knocks the coffee cup over. Dark brown splurts out and gushes across the paper, painting the song in puddle-coloured clouds.

He looks at me, wide-eyed, mouth open to shape an apology.

Still the bird sings, tinkling.

Kathryn Leigh

Seabairns

I T IS A HARBOUR TOWN, A SEA TOWN. Facing east, so dawn breaks orange over the sea each morning and casts a strange light over the crooked buildings. The pier stretches out into the water, bleached pale and worn by years of footsteps, the quayside's skeletal limb. In the autumn, the sails gather in the bay like white homing birds. The streets are built of steps, and the jumbled houses cling to the cliffside, washing lines looping back and forth, clothes stiffening in the salt air as townsfolk scurry in between. Perched at the highest point above them, the ancient church chimes out every hour. The keystone set above its driftwood door washed up on the shore like everything else; at high tide the bells ring high, at low tide low. It is a sea town, and she won't let them forget it.

Marvell was not from the coast, not a drop of salt blood in her. She did not care for the sea or the people who come from it. *Seabairns*, she would say with a curl of the lip, whenever she first saw the boats congregating. She thought they were superstitious, with their bone dice and lucky black ship's cats and star-gazing. She mistrusted their vagrant seafaring ways; there was nothing Marvell treasured more than a hearthside and four solid walls. *A creaking hull is no home,* she would say, *and they come here in the winter, for what? Treacherous people.* They called themselves the sea's children, and they worshipped their mother with a steady fervour; the idea of it made Marvell want to kiss her crucifix. Each day, she left the house with her eldest daughter Hale to work a stall. Even then, the land market hadn't been held in the square for a generation: the town was growing, and by then the sea market filled the cobbles by itself. So from her place outside the public house Marvell sold vegetables, still earthy, and flowers from inland. She snipped off the bases at a sharp diagonal before placing them in basins of fresh water. Her daughter bound the flowers with sea-green eyes.

It was an overcast afternoon. The church bells had rung three times and gulls began to alight on the roofs along the main street, knowing the workday was done. Marvell took down the striped awning and threw the flower water into the gutter, as across the street Old Matt complained he had never seen a tide lower than today's. Her daughter put the last rose rescued from the stall through her buttonhole.

Who else's daughter is so lucky? A corsage just from working, her mother said.

Shall I fetch the children? was all Hale replied. She was as quiet as any of her mother's beloved flowers.

The schoolhouse sat three-quarters way down back then, past the square, on a street above the jetty. It was a square greenish building, and at certain times and in certain lights it seemed to fade into the sky and become invisible. Hale's brother and sister were nearly old enough to walk home alone – she was sure younger children did. But still her mother insisted, so every weekday she would head down the thousand steps with a coin in her pocket for hard sweets and a frown set on her pale face. She was pretty in a sun-bleached way – no eyebrows to speak of and hair light as hay, wistful as the creature on the prow of a shipwreck. The seamarket was bustling that day. The seabairns had arrived, with their goods and their raucous songs and their accented chatter, and the old merchants had come out to reunite with their wandering friends. Hale slipped eelish between the bodies, heading for the old woman with her crock of sweets. As she approached, there was someone standing in her way. Someone in a patched shirt and heavy boots, someone who also wore the smell of the sea. He had very dark hair and carried a small child that clamoured, in its baby bird way, for food.

I'm sorry, he said, when he caught her looking with a sullen mouth.

It's fine.

He looked at her again, she at him; she saw he wore a silver necklace, a single pearl sitting bright as an eye against his throat.

I like your necklace, she said, and she wasn't sure where it came from.

He laughed and shied away, while the child clung around his neck. *It's my grandmother's.*

Hale realised she was late. Her siblings were probably last, waiting alone with their satchels and dog-eared books.

Is that a rose? She looked down at the yellow petals blooming from her buttonhole. She wished she had worn a cleaner shirt and that her hair wasn't so windswept.

Yes.

I like it.

Are you from the sea?

Can you tell?

Well. Well, yes.

Good, he said, paying the sweet seller with a small bronze coin. *I'm glad.*

A gust washed in off the waves, chilling them both, and he turned to leave, but Hale put her hand on his sleeve. She, usually shy as those flowers that close as the moon rises.

Do you have time to spare? she asked. She was not innocent of the stares aimed at them, though he, blushing, was. Perhaps that is why he said yes.

And so, as autumn ended, a sweet companionship began. Marvell noticed the absence in her daughter's eyes and took it for boredom, wanderlust.

You'll run this stall one day, she said.

Yes, mother, Hale invariably replied, and Marvell hoped her distant child was imagining life beyond the town's edges, over the cliff top, inland. She had long wanted to return to the enclosed pocket-handkerchief fields of her youth, to escape from a town where, in her small garden, her plants shrivelled in protest at the briny soil. But Hale thought not of escape – only of a certain green-eyed boy. She thought of his salt-stiff hair, of holding him in her arms while the sea lashed against the walls of the church. The water could rise to suck around the gravestones while she kissed his face beneath the carving of Saint Michael. They would meet to share secrets on the empty beach.

Not to sound childish, she said to him one day, *but I think I like that my mother would despise you.*

Yellow-hair people are bad luck, he said. *Everyone knows that.* And they shared the dried fruit he had from across the sea and kissed the salt from each other's lips.

It ended in the evening of a calm day. The children were playing with their toy boats while Hale sat by the roaring hearth, humming something unfamiliar. From her seat across the room Marvell saw the box in her daughter's lap, suddenly noticed the earrings hung with small shells, and how the smell of the sea always clung to her skin. And then, in an instant, she recognised the lies for what they were – *the bookstore, the sweet stall, my friend's mother's baby.* In a rage she crossed the room and snatched the seabairn gift; opening it and seeing the seabairn copper chain with its single pearl. She threw it into the fireplace before Hale's horrified eyes. There must have been a piece of driftwood in among the rest, because the flames spat and flared green as the love token caught and burned. Afterwards, Hale cried bitterly, openly, and the sound was as welcome as larksong to Marvell. There would be no seabairn hands on her daughter's flesh – Hale sat high above the tideline in her mother's cruel esteem. The window was open, but only a black cat heard Marvell's fury and her daughter's sobs carried down the empty street. The younger children watched from their bedroom window that night and saw the plumes of smoke begin to drift, ever so slightly, inland. They saw on the horizon, as they fell asleep, an ominous, thickening black line.

The storm bells began to ring at high noon. Marvell sent her daughter to pick up the children as the gulls flew in off the ocean, ahead of the oily shadow that spread across its surface. She watched Hale walk away into the prevailing wind, clutching a bucket of cut roses against her chest, her shawl wrapped around her like a shroud. In the bay, the boats emptied as the sky darkened, the seabairns seeking shelter from the unforgiving weather. All along the streets doors were bolted in canon, children herded inside, firewood collected from the outdoor piles. When Marvell eventually headed home herself, awning lashed down, the storm was rising. The weather-vane quivered easterly, purple clouds roiling above the deserted alleyways, with their washing lines stripped bare as sinew. Marvell reached the house just as the first raindrops hit the cobbles.

It was darker inside than out. An unlit candle sat on the table, the flowers nowhere to be seen. There were no boots at the door, and the ashes in the hearth were cold.

Hale?

An abrupt knock at the door, and Marvell sighed in relief. She had already begun her scolding when she saw the person escorting her children was not Hale.

There's a terrible storm brewing, the schoolmistress said in disapproval.

Marvell ushered the children inside with thanks and shut the door, leaning on it as if to keep out the gale. The children looked around with fearful eyes.

Where's Hale? Marvell crossed the room, knelt down and tried to light a fire in the grate. Her hands were shaking and she scattered the matches as the wind hissed down the flue. The shutters rattled insistently, until she stood and opened the door once again to find the belligerent rain lashing down. Salt rain. She called out, but her daughter's name was snatched from her throat. Down at the seafront the waves overflowed, spilled rushing forwards and sucked back across the seamarket square, rushing to brush the bottom of the thousand steps, uprooting the small plants that grew between the cobbles there. Marvell climbed the stairs to find her daughter's room bolted from the inside.

Child!

She could taste the sea, briny, cold, and saw a trickle of green water run from beneath the locked door, past her feet and between the floorboards, down the uncarpeted stairs – a tiny river, growing wider into a torrent, until water poured as quickly as if the room beyond was overflowing with it. She howled against the door as the wind howled around the garden, as the weathervane swung ceaselessly back and forth. She was sure she heard her daughter's voice over the pounding of the sea in her ears. It was in her home, its fingers on her walls, its tongue in her hearth, and it surely relished in her fear. Her tears were saltwater, too.

Marvell looked down to find the floor inexplicably dry; when pushed the door opened with a pregnant creak. Inside, a cool merciless light. The shutters were open and trembling in the easing wind. White curtains billowed over the translucent, soaked bedsheets. She went to clutch them and found them gritty with sand, stagnant with saltwater, a drowned man's clothes and a piece of golden seaweed draped across the pillow like familiar hair. She ran it, reverentially, through her icy hands.

Outside, in the harbour, the sea, steel-grey, subsiding, returned to its natural heart-like rhythm, as the moonlight reflected silver off the sails of the boats moored there.

Shannon Lewis

Excerpts

Sunday 29ᵗʰ March, 2015

BURNED MY HAND TODAY. I DIDN'T MEAN TO, I SUPPOSE. I just settled my
hand on the hot roof of a red Ferrari for a moment. Or I thought it was a
moment. The sun was too hot and glaring. It was in my eyes. I didn't even
feel it. I only noticed when I peeled my hand off the car and it was pink and
blistering. The owner of the car, whose grocery bags I had been carrying,
had a worried look on his face. He asked me if I was OK. I didn't answer.

When I got home, I turned all the lights off and used a lighter I'd
nicked from the store to light a candle. I watched the flames furl and unfurl
on the small wick. I let them intertwine with the fingertips. I felt a vague
warmth come off them but aside from that nothing. No pain.

Huh.

Sunday 5ᵗʰ April, 2015

I have to say, I agree with TS Eliot. April is the cruellest month. In just
its first week I'm already waiting for it to end. On 1ˢᵗ April I emerged
from the store to find my bike had been spray-painted neon yellow. I
considered checking the security cameras to see who had done it but I
figured it wasn't worth the hassle. Katy from the store says I should press
charges. Whatever.

I have begun biking down Deadman's Hill. On it, there are signs
specifically outlining that biking down it is prohibited. I hear that some
kid died on it once. As I bike, the wind rushes through my hair and the
world becomes a blur and for a brief moment, I'm faster than anything and
anyone and no one can touch me. I long for the rush of adrenaline now.

It comes occasionally, when the front wheel of the bike wobbles or slips a moment, but it is muted and brief.

Mom called yesterday. She says I should take up painting. Says it's relaxing or something. "Good for the soul."

Sunday 12th April, 2015

Mom just called to tell me how proud she is of me. The painting I made won some local contest. I can't remember what for. I sent the award to my mom. I didn't even read it. I bought the paints and canvas on Monday. On Tuesday, I made a gray square on a black background with grey stripes. On Wednesday, I splashed all the colors on a white canvas and stepped on it for good measure. That one won the contest. The other one I hung in my bedroom.

I don't understand what people saw in the other painting, but they approached me with tears in their eyes. Someone offered to buy it. I didn't even care. I read somewhere that when Harper Lee published *To Kill a Mockingbird*, she was so overwhelmed by its success and by its being wrenched from her grasp that she never wrote again. I can't imagine. I sold my prize-winning painting for five dollars and left the gallery early.

Sometimes, I look at the grey painting and feel a bit sad. Well, less sad and more numb. I wish people would love that painting. But it's so drab. I can't even imagine anyone hating it. That's too strong an emotion. They'd feel more of a mild case of ennui.

Sometimes I think life is just a mild case of ennui.

I kind of wish it wasn't.

Sunday 19th April, 2015

I went on a date on Friday. Katy said Sam was great and I would have an awesome time. He got me hyacinths. I was home by 10. I've always found dating a tiresome activity. The back and forth, the flirtation, the carefully arranged display of oneself. It's a bit... dull.

It was my birthday last week. On Tuesday. I had forgotten. The only way I remembered was from an automatic email I got from the dentist reminding me about the birthday discount they now offered. 10% off.

What a deal. I think my mom forgot as well. She hasn't called in a while. I should call her soon. Check in.

Sunday 26th April, 2015

The funeral went off without a hitch. The catering company's food was good enough and they were on time. Everyone said nice things. I gave a speech about what a nice mom she was and about our weekly phone calls. In the front row, I saw Aunt Hilda wipe away a tear.

I forgot and accidentally phoned the house on Saturday. I got the answering machine. It was an automated message except the name. That was mom's voice. Should I feel bad that I didn't cry? I feel like the greyness inside me is spreading to my throat and eyes. It's choking me. Everything is tainted by it. I wish I was free.

Sunday 3rd May, 2015

I'm still trembling. I can't believe what I've done. I'm angry and sad and screaming and alive! I was in the dentist's waiting room, on the 23rd storey, staring out the window, when I heard screams below. I stuck my head out and saw a small crowd forming on the sidewalk outside. They were all staring at the roof above me. I looked up and saw a man in a suit and tie, sobbing, standing at the edge of the building. He was saying goodbye into his phone. Then he looked up, determined and strong and flaring, and let himself fall. I reached my hand out, stupidly, and caught him by the ankle. By then, the dentist had come into the room. He helped me pull the man in. I looked at the man, now pale with fear, and I felt life rush through my veins. I hugged his body and kissed his face and cried like I never have. I miss my mom! I wish she hadn't died! I wish I could fall in love! I hate that those fucking kids trashed my bike! I am not content with watching my life unfold before me!

I AM ALIVE!

I lit a candle today, in honor of my mom. My fingers lingered on the match for a bit too long and the flames bit them. I dropped the match. The flames burned me this time. It hurt.

Benjamin Lubbock

We came to know bliss

W E WERE BUT A FEW, BORN OF A MOTHER WE NEVER KNEW. Yet we came to know that, from the void before birth, to this, we came to live. Into a life we questioned since we had developed that capability of thought. Before thought, all we had was our hearing, touch and smell. With these senses we came to know one another: by the ways that we ambled, the rough feel of our flesh and fur and the individual scents that we carried. We could taste too, but that was it. There was always a feeling that our existences were incomplete. That there was a truth, hidden in the dark.

There were four of us and only four. Even in the beginning our loneliness made no sense. There was little that did. The four-walled world felt too small to be all there was. It was so empty that our hands came to recognise every rock and pebble ever since we could remember. We did not know how high the sky was; where it ended, or if. But it would drip such a constant and regular drip that we conceived and measured time by it. The air that we inhaled was heavy. It was hot and damp while the world's walls were cold with its sweat. We used to believe that these walls existed – lived – to protect us from what we did not know beyond them. We decided that there was nothing beyond them. That the walls were as dead as our bed of gravel and rocks, carpeted with dust and dirt, wet with sweat, which we inhaled in our sleep and coughed up when we awoke from the otherness. The otherness was akin to the waking world, but different. It came after the heaviness which, beginning in my head, would slow my mind and go on to spread through my body. I would crawl to a corner I could call my own where I allowed the heaviness to overcome me. In sleep, I would then enter into the otherness and I would be alone but for a voice without a body or even a mouth. It was a voice that spoke of where it came from: of somewhere beyond. I believed it when I was smaller, but grew to dismiss it as a temptation, a deception. I stopped talking about it, the others forgot

I ever had and for a long time I forgot what it had ever said to me. Instead, I woke to remember the stench which could be forgotten in the otherness. The stench, which was our own stench, only grew worse, gathered in the furthest corner. Nowhere was far enough from it.

The walls were the limits of the world and we were the limits of life within it. But there was something else with us. Something with-out us, that kept us alive. Something that stirred through the otherness, which would bring sustenance for us to eat when we woke. We awaited the fifth being, but without success. The fifth would either not come at all, or slip away with a bang. It was unlike us. Not living like us. We imagined that It was what we would become. Perhaps It was what we were before. We decided that the fifth must be our creator. That It was the first; that It was God. We came to love It. More than we loved one another, we grew to love God for the life It had given and preserved. No matter how meagre.

The world as it was was not enough for me. I had questions that obsessed me into silence; that could not be forgotten in the dark; that only God could know and which would never be answered without my asking. So I tried to trick It. Then, I was ignorant of the wrath of a God. I lay close to where the God came in. Struggling to hold of the weight of sleep, I swayed in and out of otherness. I lay still until I heard It and then rushed to embrace my creator. The flesh of God was smooth to touch, as soft as my mouth's air. I tried to speak, to ask what I needed to know, but Its voice screamed over mine. After a moment's silence, something both amazing and terrible happened: the fifth sense that hid in the dark was revealed, so bright that it broke through the lids on either side of my nose which, for the first time, opened. The brightness filled them, made them throb. In that moment I thought it was God's gift to us. I thought it was all of my questions answered before I had asked them. But all too quick, God's gift became a weapon; a beast. That was when I learnt and felt that my life was finite. Flashing teeth bit and tore at my insides and skin. It crackled, made my body burn until my fur hissed with a smell I still remember. The bright beast mauled me until it had had its fill and fled. With it, darkness fell and, with a bang, God disappeared. It abandoned me, twitching on the floor without answers. Yet with sight.

We feared God after that. Knowing God would bring sustenance, we lay as far from where It came as we could. But sleep was uneasy. An otherness came to me which repeated my encounter with God. I could explore more of the moment, see the weapon: the perfect opposite of our darkness. Before the pain, it was the most beautiful thing. It made everything it touched more than solid, but visible. It showed my hands of a lesser darkness and God's an even lesser darkness; nearly equal to the brightness. Then, the flashing agony again. I howled aloud, but woke with her holding me in her long arms, her hands gripping one of mine. She was the last, the youngest, to whom I was closest and I whispered to her about the secret of sight, about the brightness before the beast attacked. I called it Bliss. I whispered – quietly, so that not even God could hear – that I believed that the walls did not mark the world's end. To discover the beyond the voice had spoken of, I persuaded the others that we should stand against God.

Sustenance was brought and we lunged at it. Not to eat it, but to tear it, spit on it, grind it into the ground with our dust and sweat. More was brought each day, its smell growing irresistible with our starvation. But we were resilient and one day our determination proved worth our hunger. We were slumped in different corners of the world. While the others were alone, she lay with her head in my lap. I had neither the energy nor the will to reassure her anymore. I thought that I had brought the end upon us all. They who had trusted me, vowed to follow me out of the dark, were growing faint. Then, from where God would come and go, I started to see the Bliss. I held her tight, but this Bliss wasn't the same as what I had seen and felt before. Not as sharp or bright – no, it was softer, harmless. It began as a spot, grew to outline a four-walled shape. I believed that this was the way to go to the life after life. Held to my chest, I repeated the words, "it's over, it's over" in a whisper. Then the shape opened and a flood of Bliss streamed into every corner of the world. It shimmered on the wetness of the world's wall and lit the dripping sky. It flowed, warming our flesh and parted the pair of lids which withheld sight behind them. Instead of the darkness, we were blinded by Bliss. Its intensity subsided and a way out was before us. Without being able to look away from it, I led her, followed by the others to the other side. We stepped into the second world which the voice had prophesied. Where there was more to touch, to smell and to hear. With first true sight, we were born again, at last, in afterlife. With first sight of her I felt another kind of Bliss within.

We roared and beat our chests, we hugged, we wept and I held her. We saw our hairy bodies and laughed as our surroundings settled. Then I saw them and they were many, raised above us on a platform. I pointed and my friends stopped and followed my finger. They stood upright, with that flesh as smooth as my mouth's air. They had almost no hair apart from on their heads; some had hair on their faces. All were dressed in robes, gleaming in the Bliss, emitting from long strips set upon the sky. The Gods were smiling. As one, we lowered our heads to the floor, humbled by the blessing of afterlife and sight. They looked down at the tablets that they held and started moving their hands across them.

We went on to live out our afterlives in the world of sight. We ate well and danced; we lived, and yet the world was not much larger than the last. Still there were walls. Walls we could not see, behind which the Gods would walk and watch. Walls as hard as those that had kept us in the dark world. The entrance to it was always there, a shadow on the face of a rock which we would never go near. We discovered our names. I was called Wun and she was Fore. Together we made our daughter, much to the Gods' satisfaction, who named her Fyv.

I had not felt the flesh of a God since the time I first saw. We had been taught not to touch them. On occasion, a male God with fur on His face would come and He would induce sleep. Whoever He chose would collapse and we would watch as He studied our friend, looking from His tablet to the body on the floor. When the God left we would wake our friend. This God came soon after Fyv was born and did the same to her. I saw my daughter lying lifeless on the floor. I was still as He lifted her into His arms and began to walk away. But when I saw her fingers swaying at His side, something stronger than the otherness awoke within me. I only remember running and roaring her name, followed by the flashing agony.

I still see her – but only in the otherness. From which I wake to realise that I was embracing nothing but darkness.

Adam Maric-Cleaver

The propeller

W E LEAVE THE BODY UNDER THE PIER and walk back to the car. By tomorrow, high tide will take the body and it will be washed quite a way down river before anyone notices it. They won't track it back to us, Thurman says, because all the DNA and fingerprints will be washed off in the river. I know that can't be right, but it comforts me still.

Muller gets in the back of the car with his arm around Sharon's waist. I get in after them. Thurman gets in the passenger seat and tells Hunt, who is staring forward and sweating, to get a fucking move on. Hunt turns to him slowly and Thurman hits him.

"Get a move on, you fucking nigger."

We all shout a little now and Hunt puts the car in gear. It's a small old thing, but it moves off smoothly enough.

Hunt is a black. Thurman hates blacks. Muller and I are okay with them, but Thurman has a deep-seated hatred of the blacks. He's not a Nazi or anything. He's got nothing against the Jews or the Chinese or the Indians. But he can't stand blacks, so it is strange that he hired Hunt for the job today. Perhaps he knows Hunt is scared of him so he won't talk.

Sharon puts her head on Muller's shoulder next to me. Muller reaches up and grabs one of her tits in response, kneading it between his fingers through her dress. She looks down at his hand but doesn't stop him. About five minutes later, with the light coming up stronger over London, they start necking.

"Quit it, you two," says Thurman.

"Come on, Thur. We killed the arsehole hours ago."

Thurman turns in his seat to face Muller, whose face is all covered in purple lipstick and bite marks.

He says: "A few hours doesn't mean anything to God. Now we keep respectful for a day. That's the way it always is. Ain't that right?"

Hunt says: "Yes sir," and Thurman hits him again, says he was talking to me.

"I don't know. I got nothing against it." I gesture at Sharon's purple lips.

Muller seems happy that he now outnumbers Thurman. Sharon hasn't said anything.

Thurman says: "It don't matter what you think. God doesn't care what you think, does he? Now, you two: quit it."

Muller slumps back in the seat. I look out the window and see the river as we cross a bridge. In the glass I can see that Muller has got hold of Sharon's tit again.

Gabriel was always saying: "No man is an island."And I would say: "Stop talking shit."

Gabriel wasn't a talkative guy. When we used to fuck about in the evening at the pub or club, he was the one who insisted he buy the drinks and then would spend too long at the bar. Often he'd go off without checking what anybody wanted, but he'd come back with the right drinks anyway. Then he would sit with his pint and not say anything unless someone looked right at him and asked his opinion.

The question was often: "Would you?"

Gabriel would look shocked, though he'd been following the conversation. "Yeah. From behind."

And then he was back in his pint glass.

But he used to say that no one existed or acted independently.

"No man is an island."

"What about a man who lives alone on an island?"

"How did he get there?"

"His parents sent him away in a basket."

"Then his parents decided part of his life for him, didn't they?"

Gabriel was always being called sensitive, but he wasn't anything of the sort. He was just quiet and full of metaphors.

This was not why I had to get Thurman to kill him.

The reason I called Thurman was because I realised that Gabriel was the reason that everyone in the entire world was unhappy. For one thing, he had a pansy's name, which he insisted on being called. It was not Gab, Gabe, Gabby or even Gabster. It was Gabriel. Everyone is proud of stupid things, but Gabriel was proud of things that kept him from people. Nobody wanted to call him that name. Nobody wanted to know about the posh beers he had or the capital cities of countries. Nobody wanted to go for a walk after a pint. Nobody wanted Gabriel.

But Gabriel knew this and hated it and wouldn't often say so to me, say that he wanted everyone to like him, at any cost. Still, he never changed. What he really wanted was for the world to shape-shift, to become accustomed to him.

And so I had to pick a side, Gabriel or the world. Gabriel was my friend, but I had better friends. My better friends were on the side of the world.

We are in Thurman's room. Hunt has left us. Thurman shouted at him as we got out of the car, something about Hunt not waking up if he said a word. Hunt drove off without saying anything.

"Last time I use that Nigger cunt." Thurman said.

Thurman's room has only a sofa, a telephone and a propeller hung on the wall from a thin chain, like a necklace. This is where I had come to see Thurman, when I understood that Gabriel couldn't go on, that there had to be an end to him and I would have to put a stop to him myself or, I suppose, with Thurman's help.

Muller got dropped off at his house, but Sharon came back with us. She needed Thurman to give her some money he owed her. Sharon is as middle-class as anything and, as such, is a money-lender among our crowd. Thurman may have been psychotic, but even he didn't like to cross Sharon about money.

Thurman goes to the sofa, looks under it and takes out three twenty-pound notes and hands them to Sharon.

"You owe me a hundred."

"I'll have to go out to get the rest."

"You've got some under there."

Thurman doesn't respond but leaves the flat grumbling.

I am on the sofa, staring at the propeller. Sharon comes and sits next to me.

"You know, you should probably talk about it."

I turn to her and then look back at the propeller.

"No. And you aren't a fucking therapist."

"No, but you should talk about it all the same."

"You knew him too."

"Not like you. You know we thought you two were fags, the amount you two were together."

This is not how I remember it. I put my hand on her back.

"I'm not a fag."

"Good."

I am not sure why, but I feel a need to rip Sharon out of her dress. She puts her head on my shoulder.

"Muller's a lump of shit. Him and Thurman. One day, I'm going to beat the living shit out of the two of them. Won't end well for me, knowing them, but I'm going to give them a seeing-to. Especially Muller," she says.

"Why are you with him?"

"No idea."

"Why are you doing this?"

"I want to. I want to forget. So do you."

I think about pushing her head off of my shoulder, but leave it and watch the propeller, imagining it moving round, each blade chasing the other and getting no nearer.

"Do you feel better, now he's gone?"

"No."

"Worse?"

"Fuck off, Sharon."

Thurman walks in without warning. He sees us and, before we can stop him, begins to speak about God and respect for the dead.

"You know what he does? He sends down an angel and he takes note of all your sins."

"Is that all?" Sharon says, though she has shifted to the other end of the sofa, as though waiting for Thurman to sit between us.

"No. Then, when you die, the angel shows you heaven. You see it all and then he takes you to hell."

I can't see the propeller because Thurman is in the way, so I get up and move past him. He turns round and grabs my shoulder.

"Sit down."

I hover round the propeller and then snatch it off the wall, like a moth finally crashing into a light bulb. I cradle it.

When I turn around Thurman has pulled a knife on me, a short, curving affair. It doesn't frighten me as much as it should.

"Put down my propeller."

"What do you need it for?"

"I like to look at it."

"Where did you find it?"

"Put it down."

"Where did you find it?" I say again, blank. I have disconnected myself from the knife and the room and Sharon and Thurman. For this reason, if nothing else, I must now have the propeller.

"I found it on the river, at low tide. Probably off a boat."

Good. From far away, I think.

For a moment, I feel a lot better, but I accidently catch Sharon's eye. She mistakes the rising hope in my eyes for a signal – of love or action, I can't quite tell. Either way, she throws herself at Thurman, biting and beating on him. He turns quickly and slashes without thought, cuts her right across the front. She comes at him again, this time kicking. But he's ready for that and gets her good again with the knife. I watch, floating on the propeller's current. Eventually, Thurman says: "One last chance. Then you go in the river."

Sharon looks at me, betrayed. I look down at the propeller. From far away. Sharon must have tried something again, because I hear a struggle.

There is a lot of screaming for a time before she passes out.

"You can keep the bloody propeller. Phone Joe, I'll need him for her." He points to Sharon, who is breathing lightly.

"After that, get out. And don't call me."

I phone Joe and leave.

The propeller watches from my table, chasing itself. Gabriel would know why I need it. Maybe that is why I need it. Sharon didn't make it. Hunt ratted on Thurman and as he and Joe were leaving the house with Sharon, the police were all around the place and took them all in. But Hunt only gave Thurman's name and address, or at least that's what I think, as I haven't heard from the law. I saw Muller too. He asked me where Sharon was. Then he said something about Gabriel. I think of them both, far-off and cold, but still lingering in some way, like corroded debris.

Isabel Martin

Patient

I.

YOU ENTER THE PARK. The gate swings shut behind you, the guttural clank of metal on metal resonating through your skull. How many times have you walked through that gate? Thousands, probably. But you never noticed until now how loud it was.

You need a rest, a break, a chance to get out of the house. Not that you do much any more, so you're not sure what exactly it is you're taking a break from. Still resting. The change of scene doesn't seem to have had much of an effect on you. You're just cold.

Kids are on the pitch that you and your mates trampled at their age. Scruffy-haired boys with muddy shins, their names and faces long forgotten now. The children shriek into the sunset, their silhouettes chasing the black dot that bounces across the grass.

A dog charges past you, Frisbee caught between its jaws. You had a dog once, but it died. Cancer.

Your mother told you it was sent to live on a farm. You were four, and you believed her.

You wanted to live on the farm too, you decided.

You watch the dog recede into the distance.

You locate an empty bench. Sit down. Breathe. Groan, as quietly as possible.

You taught kids here once, when you volunteered at the holiday camp. They boasted about your contributions years later.

A woman passes you, toddler hanging on to her hand. She glances back at you over her shoulder and you grit your teeth. She recognises you, but she can't quite place you.

You close your eyes. The light makes your head throb. You don't spend much time in the sunshine any more.

"Mummy, why is that man asleep?"

"Don't point, darling, it's not polite."

You do not open your eyes. You listen to the child's voice piping away down the path, staring into your eyelids. You stare for so long that you forget the blackness is there; it merges into one blind spot. Maybe this is what death looks like.

The pain is still sawing at your brain, but the medication would just make it worse. It clouds your head, stops you thinking straight.

You hear the battering of wings, and open one eye. A seagull has stopped to investigate, but takes off once you shift position. There in one breath, then gone.

You wish you'd brought a jacket. You wonder how long you have to spend here for it to "do you good".

Your phone buzzes, but you ignore it. The kids from the pitch are filtering out of the gate now, and the day has dimmed. You contemplate standing up. You groan internally. You heave yourself to your feet. Your legs never used to shake like this. You look at the empty football pitch. You sigh. You walk away.

2.

I keep tripping because the floor is all squeaky and slippy. Mummy hasn't been in any of the rooms; I think she went home in the car and left me, maybe. She will be cross because I ran away. I didn't mean to be naughty but the needle was massive and I didn't want it in my arm, all sharp and digging. Maybe I missed my injection time and I can go home now. She said it isn't meant to hurt you, it's to protect you against nasty diseases. But it can't be good if it hurts, so I think maybe she made a mistake.

There's posters with people looking worried and there's funny words and sometimes the people look happy maybe because the doctor made them better but it's all wrong because I'm lost and they're laughing at me.

I want to shout out for her but I might start crying and then they will laugh at me and I can't cry because I'm not a baby; I'm five and I have to find her before the hospital closes and I get locked in.

My throat is all funny and hot, like my breath is trying to run away, and I feel all watery and like I want to make a big noise but I can't; I can't.

There's footsteps but they're like shuffling, Mummy's feet go tap tap tap.

"Are you all right, sweetheart?"

That's a lady and she's smiling at me, I haven't seen her before but I think she's a doctor because she has a card with her picture on it and she's wearing the funny necklace they use to listen to your heart. I don't think she's meant to be wearing it now; maybe she forgot to take it off. I have to be careful in case she secretly has a needle in her pocket but I don't think I will mind if she listens to my heart, I just don't want a sore poked arm.

She asks me if I am lost and I nod my head yes. She holds my hand like Mummy does and that makes me feel sad but I don't know why. She takes me to a big desk and there is Mummy looking all messy and annoyed like when she's trying to do work and I want to play. When she sees me she makes this big breath like the wind going *whoooo* and shakes my shoulders but not hard, and then she gives me a hug and I can feel my chest going back to normal. Like something was squeezing all the time but now it's letting me go. She says: you had me worried sick. It's a funny thing to say in a hospital when there are doctors and lots of sick people. I say can we go home and she says promise me you won't run away again, and I say I promise.

3.

The waiting room is a wash of blue, a desperate reach for tranquillity: Blue chairs spilling their foam upholstery, a faded seascape hung lopsidedly on the peeling wallpaper, a chipped blue plant pot.

The plant is dying.

There is a murmur of whispered conversations, with no real reason for the hush.

Besides a stack of mismatched pamphlets, crumpled magazines are strewn across the little table in front of you: celebrity gossip of two summers ago; a torn electronics magazine; copies of *Gardening Weekly*. People steal the good ones, apparently.

Questions about cancer?

You snort, and the woman opposite you glances up.

The word patient originally meant "one who suffers". It was Greek, or Latin, or something. You don't remember.

Patience is a virtue, and yours is being worn thin. You can always rely on the doctor to be late. Have patience, patient. You almost smile.

The little girl's heels scuff the leg of her chair, dangling at least a foot above the floor. She rubs one ear of the threadbare rabbit squashed within the crook of her elbow.

"How many?"

"One's more than enough, Emily – do you want to have false teeth when you're older?"

The child sticks out her bottom lip. "Four."

"*Four?*"

"Five."

"Don't be silly, sweetheart!"

"For my age – one two three four *five*." She beams.

"I'll let you have two treats, how does that sound? Now, are you ready to be a brave girl and get your injection done?"

The mother glances at you, smiles, rolls her eyes knowingly. You stare blankly at her, and she falters, dropping her gaze. Your mouth twitches in a delayed attempt at a compensatory smile.

You wonder how many sweets you would get for being brave.

An obnoxious little ping sounds from your mobile. The tinny vibration sends sharp twinges to the back of your eyes, scraping against your sockets. Five missed calls.

People spare a thought for you every now and then, remember that you exist. The sad friend, the dying friend, the token of their pity. They think of you occasionally, think that they ought to make the most of you while you're still there. You switch off your phone, stuff it into your pocket.

Your name flashes up on the panel on the wall, as the first brutal twinge snaps at your chest. It makes your head spin, the few paces to the surgery.

You should be honest about how bad it's getting, but what good would it do? They'll just prescribe you more drugs. More and more drugs to clog the dregs of your mind. They can't save you.

You glance at the scans on the desk, the illness mapped out like spilled ink. It seems to cover most of your body at this point. You're not hearing the words spilling from the doctor's mouth. It's time to start thinking about more effective pain relief. You have to understand that these are often life-shortening, but the *quality* of life will increase significantly. We have to be thinking about balance at this time.

Will you consider the options over the week?

You want to go to bed, to lie there until your heart finally splutters to a halt.

You pass the child again on your way out, still happily babbling about sweets.

And then pain.

It is a supernova, clamping down on your heart, your head. It seizes you, gripping your chest, pummelling your brain as your legs shake, spasm, and suddenly your limbs are knocking against the floor and there is nothing but darkness, and alarms, and shrill voices, a wailing child and the thud of running feet, so many of them, and

4.

It is never an easy thing, losing a patient.

He had become numb to the fact that he was dying. He had been terminal for months. He gritted his teeth and ploughed through each day.

She knew who he was, of course. She recognised his face the first time he walked into her surgery.

She had slyly Googled his name later that afternoon.

Retired footballer, consumed by disease. If he had been in one of the bigger teams, the press wouldn't have left him alone. It's fortunate for him, really, that he retired years ago.

It's hardest for the loved ones, usually, but he has – *had* – no family that she needs to tell. She had pitied him, but in a strange, perverse way she can't help feeling that it is a blessing. It is an impossible feat, having to wrench the hope from the tear-stained relatives, having to tell them what they know already, somehow. They are the ones who will feel the weight of the loss, the blow that strikes again, and again.

He was always alone. She asked him, once, whether he would like to have somebody there with him for his next appointment. Somebody you trust, she had said. A friend, or relative, or – ? He had snorted, and she did not ask him again.

It does not feel real, not yet.

"I'm afraid Anthony has passed away," she informs the empty room.

Her gaze lingers over his file. Gently, she closes the cover.

Three strange tales of...

...

I – Los Angeles, CA
II – Silverthorne, CO
III – Roswell, NM

...

I – The Kraken sleeps

A ND BEHOLD, RISING LIKE THE VENGEANCE of a billion over-fished salmon, from the boiling, blood-warm waters of the Pacific, the Kraken wakes. In a maelstrom of writhing and thrashing tentacles *She* comes, maw agape. She is hungry.

But the last fire and the descent of the heavenly host was postponed at the last minute, so the Kraken checks herself into the Marriott on Sunset and 6th and waits, sipping Jacob's Creek from the minibar.

The sun falls in a silent flailing scream over the edge of the world. Scorched reds and burnt orange; fire tumbling into the cold, forever blue of the Pacific. In their wake the tired gold flows soft and slow over the horizon, the serenity of green dancing behind. Purple steps in, handing the day to the night with calm solemnity. It has been a long time since She saw a sunset like this. It seems a shame she won't see another.

It's nearly eleven, and tomorrow will be a big one – for it is written. Still, she can't drift into the tides of dreamless sleep. Gently mesmerized by the lazy dance of the ceiling fan, drawn into the spilled amber of the streetlights, behold, She goes out to find a bar. The Kraken has slept long enough.

And lo, it came to pass that the Kraken, vengeance of the deep, end of all things, went into *Joe's Sports Bar and Grill* and ordered a vodka slimline tonic and two wedges of lime.

It's singles' night at Joe's. By eleven, pretty much everyone's paired off: the hipsters, the yuppies, the lonely magicians looking for their one true lovely assistant. The divorcees are buying one another overpriced cocktails and projecting. *My ex-husband would never have gone somewhere like this – my kids won't believe I met someone like you – did I mention my BMW has leather seats?*

She, of whom there is one and shall forever be the Only, watches from the bar.

You poor bastards, she thinks.

Buy you a drink? he says.

He's dressed all in black. His eyes are a quiet, gentle sea-green and he's grinning nervously. Puzzled and flattered, the Leviathan of old R'lyeh says *yes*. A dozen eyelashes bat in the barlight.

The hours pass. Sean tells her about his job in a West Hollywood sex shop. They drink, they laugh, they dance to "I Want You Back" by the Jackson Five. Later they stumble out of *Joe's Sports Bar and Grill,* back to her room.

...

Red light – wrathful, brighter than a hundred suns – shines spiky through the crooked blinds. The Kraken wakes. She has a headache. Sean is nowhere to be seen. He crept out with the dawn; he left her; what a shithead. He's nowhere to be found. Rage, older than the first dawn, rises with her from the ruined sheets. Her body grows, tentacles spreading across the room. The burning of the world gleams in her cold, endless eyes – her tentacles rise like a storm about her. The hosts of heaven and hell, eager, thirsty for immortal blood; a thousand tasteless burning swords loosen in their scabbards. The end is...

A knock, tentative, cheerful on the door. It's Sean, bagels and Lox and aspirin in hand. She smiles, embarrassed. Blinds close, sheets twist, the armies of the Eternal Light and the Endless Dark wait, in their eternal rank and file, for She who shall begin the end of all things is in bed. She yawns, happy and tired. Smiling, the Kraken sleeps...

...

II – *A Light Snow Falls in the Parking Lot of the* Smilin' Moose Rest Stop and Waffle House

It had snowed lightly in the night, and again in the morning. The parking lot of the *Smilin' Moose Rest Stop and Waffle House* already filled with a dirty slush. Pickups criss-crossed the puddles and ruts, stopping to rest as long as the single, tired waitress kept up her rounds with the coffee pot. No one ever hurried to leave the *Smilin' Moose.* They hunched in booths, exchanging their mutterings. No one sat in the window seats.

The road ran up past the *Moose,* into the mountains that waited in the roiling clouds like a promise. If you stood on the roof of the outbuilding where the snow shovels, bear-proof waste bins and extra sacrificial knives were kept, you could see between the peaks of Old Tooth and Scott's Sorrow, all the way up to The Temple. If you stood there at night you could see the fires burning. And, behind those ruddy glows, stranger, colder glimmerings that danced and slithered in the dark. The ancient Wurlitzer Jukebox in the back of the *Moose* was always turned up loud at night. The rattly blare and hum of Chuck Berry records was almost enough to drown out the howl of the wind and the strange, metallic shriekings they carried with them.

The Boy did not stand on top of the outbuilding that looked up between the peaks to The Temple. He stood, leaning against the grey brick wall, looking at nothing in particular. Hot air from the open kitchen door warmed the back of his neck. The tip of his nose was already numb in the cold. His apron, soaked and stained with dishwater, steamed gently. The tip of his crinkled roll-up flared; smoke mingled with the steam in his breath: it coiled into the leaden sky. As they had on his previous two smoke breaks today, the Boy's thoughts turned, inexorably, to the dream. Not a vision of wet stone walls lit by sickly green light and a hooded figure beckoning with a single, effeminate finger (everyone had those). No. There had been *Golden light... a city in the clouds... and the beautiful figures who wore no hoods...* he couldn't for the life of him remember their faces, but he remembered the things they had said, had asked him to do. The boy shivered. No one could know. No one would believe him... and if they did... he shivered.

The half-smoked cigarette hissed into the dirty slush by the back door.

The Boy returned to his sink. Inky clouds curled and prowled between the peaks. In the parking lot of the *Smilin' Moose Rest Stop And Waffle House,* a light snow began to fall.

...

III – *The First and Last Cosmic Gift Shop*

The lights are brighter than ever tonight; an Endless indigo blanket; diamonds spilled and scattered, wider than the edges of the eye. The cacti crack open Pabst Blue Ribbons and watch the sky. The lights are brighter than ever tonight. *Roswell, New Mexico. Population: 48,611. Area code: 575 ... The number you are calling is currently unavailable, please hang up, give up, don't try again.*

She switches on the sign – *Fizz, zap* and *hummmmm...* goes the ancient neon – pink-green-gold-blue-pink-red-pink... *Flap, clunk* and *creak,* goes the old folding deck chair. She rustles the pages and, under her breath, under the lights that are brighter than ever tonight: *Come and get 'em while they're hot, rhyme rhythm and verse for all, contributions voluntary, all currencies accepted* the sign screams into the night.

The Patrice Martinez Cicada Show Band of New Mexico counts off and jams, ragging and riffing through the same old songs. The conductor waves his legs. Everybody waves their legs. *Babum-cha-be-boo-doo-tsss ...* Clap along cacti –*Snick* – Goes her Arnold Palmer. *Slurp–*

Whooosh... Just a car. Settle down. No one's come before; no reason they'll come tonight... But ... The lights are brighter than ever tonight.

Behind razorwire and chainlink and the tumbleweed guards they dance, swooping back-forth-up-down-around again, all for her amusement she thinks. Condensation from the can clings to her hand, ink bleeds when you touch its paper; into to the discount bargain bin they go. Can't expect full price if it's smudged and soggy. She re-folds her legs, can in hand – *Slurp* – and returns to putting pen to page, pinning down her world for the consumption of the tourists: the first cosmic gift shop.

This little one's about a boy from Ohio. He meets the alien Quargleflorb on Christmas Eve. He takes him inside and proudly shows him the stockings and the milk and the carrots and all the presents jumbled up beneath the tree. Quargleflorb smiles and drinks his eggnog and gets in his ship to go home – where he tells everyone on *&JUI#6 about the warrior people of Earth and how they decorate the corpses of their enemies with trinkets and baubles and display them in their homes to mark their victories in bloodthirsty conquest. By an unfortunate coincidence, Quargleflorb's neighbouring planet - which by another coincidence is called Steve – is populated entirely by a benevolent race of creatures who, in addition to being great lovers of art, music and interpretive dance, also bear a striking resemblance to Douglas Firs. Overcoming our cultural differences is the key, she thinks. *Slurp* – Pen down, eyes up. The lights are still dancing.

She's sitting on the roof of her father's gas station and convenience store, beaming into the night. Downstairs her dad – also a Steve – sells a man in a cheap suit the biggest cup of coffee they have. The man is CIA, maybe FBI, CDC, ABCDEFHI – definitely not a Steve, but who can say, really? He's tired, eyes red raw from keeping the white line snugly on his left tire for two hundred miles. Not far to go now to the crash site. He doesn't believe. He will.

Red lights nod goodbye to the speedbumps. *Thank you for leaving Roswell. Drive carefully. You never know what might happen.* She shifts in the chair, in the warmth of the glow, under the endless indigo night, scattered with little jewels. Some of them might be headlights. There are no tail lights in endless indigo night. *Welcome to Earth. Stay awhile. And please, folks, don't forget to visit the gift shop on your way out.*

She sits on a ragged old deck chair on the roof of her father's gas station and convenience store. Neon light flickers all around her, and she looks only at the sky or at the page. Another tan Ford Taurus pulls in for coffee and gas on the way to believe. She reaches for another iced tea. *Tap tap tap* goes the pen on the armrest of her chair. Indigo fades to black.

The lights are brighter than ever tonight.

...

Saraswathi Menon

Where the wild things go

Athithi

THE CONCRETE CLOUDS – A BURDEN UPON THE SKY, marked the first day of monsoon in Mumbai. The Kapoors' metal black gate was so tall, I couldn't see anything within the compound, I pushed the gate but –

"Who are you? Daniel Kapoor is not at home," said the security guard.

"I'm here to see Daniel's wife, Menaka. I'm her daught... I mean sister."

I shouldn't have fumbled there; she had told me time and again. Sister. That's all that I had to remember.

"Let her in," said the man in the yellow shirt. He was tall and well built, an aspiring model standing against a white BMW.

"Menaka didn't tell me she had such a pretty sister."

He smiled and two dimples appeared. I knew that I wanted to see him more.

"I'm Athithi."

"Aditi? I'm Su–"

"No, it's Athithi. Like guest in Sanskrit?"

"Ah, athithi devo bhava¹, isn't it? Well I'm Suraj. Menaka's step-son."

He put his hand forward to pull me out of my haze.

"Nice... to... meet you."

"Well, I need to leave now, but I'll see you soon?" Suraj said, getting into his car.

I nodded. I doubt Menaka would let me see anyone from this house again. I walked on with a fistful of hope and a lifetime of questions.

"I've been waiting." Menaka's wearing a black chiffon sari and six-inch heels. The red lipstick-stained mouth smiles.

1: 'The guest is to be treated like a god'– Sanskrit proverb

Police report- 24.6.2014

The villagers came to the station reporting a body in the forest. The body was in a suitcase. She was badly burned. I passed this information on to the Mumbai division.

*

Suraj

It had been a month since Athithi came to stay with us. As I passed by our lounge, I saw her silhouette against the windows stained with raindrops that her fingers were tracing. Mumbai is at its best is when it rains, relentlessly, on the lost souls colliding in this city; everyone pauses just for a minute to let the sky talk.

"Athithi?" I said, entering the room.

She flinched a little and stumbled. This wasn't the first time I'd managed to catch her slightly off-guard. Fear was her response to everything, even to my affection, which I hated. I wouldn't want to be involved with someone who shares the same blood as that vamp Menaka. Athithi was so unlike her, it made me question genetics.

"Who knew darkness could be this beautiful?" she said, turning towards me, folding up a square of paper.

I met her eyes; eyes that looked at the world so closely while the world looked away... Stop it, Suraj, stop looking at her like that. She sits next to me on the peach sofa that Menaka chose – I've always hated it.

"Do you miss home and your mom?" I ask.

"I do, but–"

"So do I."

Can you miss something you've never had – stability, perhaps?

"You're at home, though, aren't you?" she asks with half a smile; her thumb fixes the folds of the paper.

"This is a house, but I wouldn't call it home. I mean, my real mom is on a painter's retreat in France, my brother's abroad, and dad's barely here."

"You mentioned you've moved a lot? A wanderer?" she asks.

"When you've grown up caught in a custody tug-of-war, it's not really a choice."

"Your choice, you mean. I believe everything is chosen for us."

For some reason, this didn't sound so naïve when she said it. What was it about her? I didn't dislike everything as much when she was around?

"Here you go." She gave me a paper house, two slanting planes that slid down to join four white walls.
"A paper house?"
"No, a home, a portable one for the wanderer."
"Why?"
"Because no one should feel like they don't have a home."
And then I knew I wanted her.
"Have you been out for a drive in Mumbai?"
She looked confused.
"You haven't? Well, I decided that 2013 for me would be a year of spontaneity. So I think we should take the car for a spin... Now," I suggested.

*

Police report- 3.3.2015

The Mumbai division called our district. They asked about the body we found last year. An anonymous phone call tipped them off.

*

Menaka

When I saw Athithi, I could see Arnav's grey eyes staring at me as I slept long after he had gone. Whenever I take off my bangles, I remember the texture of his coarse palms, pressing against my wrists to pin me down.
"Do you think you're better than me? I'm a man, I get what's mine," he said.
Men don't understand rejection; Indian mothers bring them up with a sense of over-entitlement. I didn't hate Athithi, but I didn't love her. I wasn't ready for a baby yet. I was seventeen.
My mother hated me because of the pregnancy. Yet I never let her forget that she was responsible for letting Arnav into the house. She left me in his care as she travelled with her second husband. He was my cousin, he wanted to marry me. I rejected him, that scumbag.

She thought she was oh-so-smart for letting us "spend time together".
He never came back because he didn't want anything to do with the child.
How fucking convenient. For women, our body is a curse. Men make the
mistakes, and we learn to endure. I wasn't going to let that happen.

I was destined for greater things. The way boys looked at me in school, I
knew I could get them to do what I wanted. But how was I meant to get
them to look at me if I had a screaming child on my hip? So needy, they eat
and cry and puke and suck the life out of you. Infants are nothing but
small human parasites.

No one needed to know about Athithi. She lived in a world that made
sense, one with my parents. Not with me, this penthouse, my empire – I
mean, Daniel funds it but I run it. My mother said Athithi accidentally
saw the birth certificate. Yeah, I'm sure. I'm surprised my mother even
held a lie within her so long. Must have been churning inside her; no
wonder she has a kidney problem.

Athithi came looking for me because of that, she claims. Athithi likes
mom better than I do; maybe because she got it right the second time.
Perhaps she fixed herself after all.

*

Police report- 24.4.2015

*This body could be related to a missing person's report about the sister of
industrial tycoon Menaka.*

*

Athithi

After I found out that Menaka was my mom, I wanted to be just like her:
stunning, sharp and sophisticated. I never thought I was as attractive but I
hoped Suraj thought so. I'm not sure, and I don't think Menaka would like
it at all if I liked Suraj or he liked me. Which will never happen.

All those years, away from home, I had wondered if she thought about
me. When I first found out that I had another mother, a "real" mother, I
was confused and angry. Why didn't anyone tell me? Did I not deserve to

know or was I never meant to know? I don't know what is worse.

Ma – or should I say grandma? – became so ill but while looking for medicine, I found the birth certificate. The truth. Then, I decided to go and meet Menaka because grandma needed money and I needed answers.

*

Police report- 16.6.2015

After the post-mortem was carried out, the DNA evidence suggested that the deceased was not Menaka's sister but her biological daughter.

*

Suraj

It had been five months of Athithi and me. We sat on the end of marine drive, waiting for twilight to immerse itself in the sea for us to unleash the stories of our sins. She placed her fingers over mine when I told her about that scar on my left arm. People rarely asked about it, and when they did, I lied. If she was someone else, I wouldn't have revealed the truth, but it was her. I had to tell her.

The halo of city light spilled on to her face as she withdrew her fingers and turned towards the skyscrapers that were scattered with white squares.

"What is it, Athithi?"

She sniffled.

"I don't know," she said.

"Don't know what?"

"How to stop liking you."

"Who said you had to?" I said.

She leaned towards me. I couldn't help but want to kiss her. She didn't resist. Cars went past us and took away the ghosts of our scars.

*

Police report- 16.9.2015

Blunt force trauma, just as I expected. The motive of the murder is yet to be determined but I presume it is a crime of passion.

*

Menaka

It was all Daniel's fault. He insisted that Athithi should stay in our house till she finished her masters here. Now Suraj and Athithi want to move in together and get married and before you know it, inherit this empire that I've worked for. She didn't come to find me, but to avenge what I did to her. I wasn't going to let her do that. Her affection was just a façade.

And she enters my room.

"How could you?" I ask.

"I could because you did. You left me, and now I found you but you don't want me but Suraj does and because of that I'll keep seeing you and maybe you'll love me, not as a daughter but as your daughter-in-law. Because you have to. You'd do anything to seem nice in front of Daniel."

I couldn't believe what she had just said.

"Well, you've ruined your chances now," I say.

"Like I even had a chance! You never realised that there is some of you in me. Could you not love me for those parts at least? Do you care for anything aside from your stolen wealth? This corrupt empire?"

"Are you threatening me?"

"No, I'm just reminding you of the person that you are," she said.

I moved closer to her.

"Oh. Who is that?" I ask.

She looks at me intensely –

"A whore... a vulture, like Suraj said."

That's it, that bitch. I slap her hard and she hits the glass table.

*

Menaka

The blood on the sink, the guilt in my veins, dead daughter in our master bedroom. I couldn't hide it from Daniel. He covered his mouth with his fingers. He looked at me, and for the first time I saw no love.

*

Police report- 19.8.2015

After the industrial tycoon, Menaka, killed the victim, Athithi, she used her phone to make it seem like she was still alive. Did anyone believe those messages?

*

Suraj
"Do you know where the wild things go, they go along and take your honey..." [2]

Athithi's favourite Alt-J song is playing in the bar that we used to visit. Without the vultures and the drama.

"Sir, the cheque," says the bartender.

As I am searching for my wallet in my sports bag, I can feel my thumb sink into paper. Home, our paper home. I promised her that I would take it with me wherever I went. I can still feel the impressions of her nails when I touch the creases.

She texted me saying that she never loved me and it was all an act. I didn't believe it; I had to call the police without Menaka's knowledge. Daniel and Menaka tell me that she left to travel the world. I think something went wrong, really wrong. Where did you go, Athithi? Why didn't you take me with you? The wanderer is homeless, once again.

*

2: Breezeblocks' by Alt-j, 'An Awesome Wave', Infectious Records, 2012.cc.

Saraswathi Menon

Diazepam

Chocolate chip lips. After dark tongue. Windows down.Streetlights are the golden
dolphins that swim with us as you accelerate past the night. Our summers, the sun, the
moon and
> when you said and when I said: *I love you.*

Old lovers lurking in our backyard. New friends that I have not met. Our kisses drizzle, just for the parties. Our monsoons, the sun, the moon and when you said and when I said: *Who is that?*

Darting through my brain, those messages. Words like parasites on our sanity. When do we even speak? Our winter, the sun, the moon and when you said and when I said: *I will leave you.*

You see, I'm child of paranoia – my mother, jealousy and my father, anxiety – and when they both fuck, it's usually when they're angry. That's how they got me.

Ciara Moran

The old new house

THE BOY HAD ALWAYS ENJOYED CAR RIDES. He liked to think about the similarities between the hum of the car engine and the purring of a lion. He imagined that he was in a bubble, freshly blown and trailing along on the wind, watching everything as he went past. Sometimes, the car was the boy's own spacecraft, thrust forward by the momentum of turbo-jets. Other times, it was a suitably impenetrable nest, in which he could sleep and feel safe. There was nothing quite like watching the endless flow of street lamps on the motorway home at night, each one blending and dissolving as it went by, leaving behind a leaked trail of light for the rest to grip on to. Sometimes he asked his mother to take him for a ride, just because the car was one of his favourite places to be.

That day, the boy and his mother had packed their lives into boxes, stripping bare the bones of the only home he'd ever truly known. The boy's bedroom became an empty snail shell, having once held all that his delicate life amounted to. The precious things from his shelf were now hidden among stacks of cardboard; the stars on the ceiling were all pulled down. His green spotty wallpaper was the only remaining clue, for a non-existent detective, that he had ever been there at all. The boy felt strange as he helped his mother to carry the boxes out of the house on Chiswick Street. They just about managed to fit them all into the small, slightly battered, silver Ford.

As it turned out, the boy and his mother were leaving quite a lot behind them.

...

The car journey on this occasion was certainly not as exciting as most. The boy had managed to squash himself up among the mighty pile of boxes that had eaten up the back of the car, and he wasn't particularly comfortable. He had never left so much behind him before. While his mother insisted that the change would be a good thing, he was afraid that this time she might be wrong. He was realising that while journeys to uncertain destinations can be adventures, they can also be scary.

This particular journey stretched and warped in time; one moment they had seemingly been travelling for hours and the next it had only been a short while. Then eventually the city outside the window disappeared and everything went green. The boy turned his head into the soft, worn leather of his seat.

"Don't be so down," his mother said. "We'll be there soon."

"But I won't know what it's like being there. I won't remember."

"Of course you will. Just like riding a bike. You can't forget something like that."

"But I never learned it in the first place," he said. "You have to learn things before you can remember them."

"I don't always think that's true. You can remember a sense of things. I showed you the photographs often."

"He was in them."

"He was."

"But he won't be there, with us."

"Perhaps that is just how we will know it is over."

...

His mother adjusted her seat, glancing at a blue Fiat in the wing-mirror. The boy watched the hills roll out, on and on.

"He loves me, and you," he said.

"I love you and me. Just the two of us."

"But you won't love him as well."

"I couldn't find the space to," she said. 'You're getting big enough to fill it all up."

"I could squash up a bit; I'm not that big yet."

"You have all the space you need. I want you to."

The boy shut his eyes and the hills melted away.

"There, maybe you should sleep a while. You must be getting tired."
"I think I might like the garden."
"I think you will love it. I brought your ball."
"Do you promise it will feel like ours?"
"It will,' she said. 'It is just for us."

...

The boy and his mother arrived at the house. It was small and old and it had a funny smell that meant nobody had lived there for a long time. They took off their shoes at the door and set about pretending that the place wasn't so strange to them. The boy thought the house looked too different to the old one, but he said nothing.

For dinner that evening his mother made him tomato soup from a can; it was his favourite bright orange kind. Then she started to talk about "bedtime soon" and how he would need his rest. There was a new school to go to here – as if going to regular school wasn't bad enough – and he was to start tomorrow.

"You don't need to worry," his mother said. "You'll settle in just fine, I know it." The boy recognised the worry in her voice. He smiled, despite his uncertainty, because he knew his mother loved him very much and wanted things to be good.

"I'm excited," he said, and it was possibly the first ever lie he would tell to spare her feelings.

...

"I can't sleep," said the boy, as he stood in the doorway of his mother's new room that night. She couldn't sleep either, but she said nothing. Instead, his mother lifted up her duvet cover just enough for a small person to slip inside.

"We've had a big day," she soothed. "You've had a lot to think about.'
"Don't you think about lots too?"
"Well, of course I do. I never stop."

The boy wondered how she managed to hold it all in so well, and decided it was a skill he needed to learn.

...

School was loud compared with the small house. On the playground there was nothing but other children chatting and running and shouting. However, the boy was not as alien there as he had expected. Everyone wanted to know his name. They wanted to know what games he liked, and if the schools in London smelled like smoke and if he had ever seen the Queen up close. It was a much smaller school than his old one had been; everyone there was from the same village, and when they found out that the boy was living in the house on the hill their interest in him only increased.

"I heard that a witch lived in that house, a hundred years ago," said Jess, a girl whose dad worked in the post office, "and she was extra evil."

"My mum said that when she was young she saw a scary man looking at her through the window there," said Peter, who lived next door to the post office.

"Well my brother dared me to knock on the door once, and when I did it I heard somebody coming, even though it was empty," said Shane, who had a runny nose. Everybody looked to the boy with wide, curious, and in some cases pitying, eyes. The truth was that he hadn't noticed anything spooky so far. His mother had told him it was nana's old house. But they were all looking at him so expectantly. So open to whatever it was he was going to say. He had to give them what they wanted.

"I saw a ghost in the hallway last night," he said, and he felt his insides shift with the discomfort of another lie. "It stared at me and it had glowing eyes and I wasn't *even scared*." The other children were all listening, enthralled. Occasionally they whispered to one another with morbid amazement, and in that moment, the boy became a person of great interest to the rest of class four.

...

A week passed and the stories didn't stop coming. One day it was an apparition in the mirror, the next it was the sound of footsteps down the corridor at night. He saw ghostly figures of men, women and children. Some screamed and cursed, others stared with eyes deep and dark as the starless parts of space. The boy had always had a vivid imagination, and the stories were exactly what the children wanted to hear. They made the hairs prickle at the backs of their necks, they made them weary of walking down corridors alone, and yet they still begged him for more. They loved the thrill of learning the secrets of the old house on the hill. The boy had started a profitable trading arrangement, and in exchange for his stories they gave him their approval.

The problem was that everything was starting to get to the boy too. His new bedroom was big and still needed some work; he and his mother had been so busy settling in that they hadn't finished unpacking everything yet. The creaky floorboards at night started to make him anxious. The countryside surrounding the house was too quiet; he was accustomed to the noises of cars driving by his window. The sound of their wheels on the road like waves hitting the shore. Here the main sound was that of occasional wind whooshing past the window panes, catching at branches of trees and making them dance like wild things. Eventually, he was at a point where he would sit up in his bed at night, scraggly stuffed rabbit clutched to his chest, blankets pulled to his chin, and only sleep when exhaustion got to him first. It didn't matter that the ghosts hadn't appeared yet – he was so convinced they were coming. The small house seemed too big for just two people; it was still missing a piece.

...

The boy hadn't been sleeping well for a few days. He lost concentration in his lessons at school. The other children were beginning to tire of the ghost stories, but the boy's mind was still brimming with them. Now at lunch they wanted to play tag or girls catch boys or bulldog. The teachers were starting to express concerns about him, but still the boy did not tell anyone about his anxieties. He was not a baby, after all; he was supposed to be fine. When his mother collected him that Friday, Mrs Higston asked to speak to her. The boy didn't stop worrying about what she had said for the whole drive home.

...

That evening his mother was distracted; she was constantly checking her phone and looking at her watch. She made him three fish fingers and peas for dinner, and he couldn't finish them. When he was finally tucked up in bed, the boy began to prepare for what was now his routine. He reached down into the depths of the blankets for his rabbit, and when he found it a noise caught his attention. There was a whoosh followed by a bang from downstairs. There was another solid moment of quiet, during which the boy's entire body became as heavy as lead. His heart was thrumming so hard in his chest he felt like an alarm clock that at any second was about to start ringing.

Then began the heavy steps on the stairs: slow at first and then faster. They made it to the hall, making every single floorboard creak along the way. Until finally, finally, after an agonising few minutes or moments of sheer dread, whatever it was arrived outside his door. It cast a long foreboding shadow into the room. The boy tried again to be brave, but he was now too immersed in his terror.

"Ben," said a voice. A very familiar voice. The boy lifted his face from his rabbit's fur, and there was a man. One he'd been so badly yearning for, and afraid of missing, and he'd been *afraid* to admit these things to anyone. His father stood in the doorway. He had missed him, and not one ghost story had been scarier than the boy's fear that his father wasn't coming back for him. The boy began to cry.

Jenny Moroney

The frozen lake

I T IS REBECCA WHO CONVINCES SARAH that pushing their paralysed father across the frozen lake will work out absolutely fine. Rebecca tells Sarah to be logical: going around would mean more than an hour of walking to get back to their parents' home. Their morning has been spent on a trip to the chemist for their father's medicine; they brought him with them in an attempt to get him out of his mood.

Their first steps on to the ice let out tenuous chinking noises, stopping them in their tracks. But then the thought of their elderly mother waiting for them back at the house makes them edge further out. Soon their steps are more confident; they can see they are only leaving small, surface-level cracks and their father's wheelchair glides along smoothly. They look up at the arch of pearl sky above. Squinting, Rebecca takes her sunglasses out of her coat's top pocket and puts them on before she says: "I read somewhere it's been so cold for so long that the lake is frozen right to the bottom."

"Well, just know if he wakes up I'm blaming you."

"God, he'll probably have a heart attack, won't he?"

The sisters both laugh, then their father lets out a wheezy cough which makes them quiet again. He seems to crumple in his wheelchair, the collar to his coat roughly turned up like a fence patrolling his neck. The side of his mouth is slightly open and lets out a trail of steam into the crisp air. Watching him, Rebecca snorts and says: "Remember when he used to have that pipe?"

"Yeah, mum would find the ash in little piles around the house."

Rebecca sighs and adjusts her sunglasses. "Why did she ever put up with him?"

Sarah smiles, squeezing her gloved fingers round the metal handles of the wheelchair. "I suppose she loves him."

"No I don't think that's it. Otherwise she'd have been more bothered by it all. She just never had another option."

"She still looks after him now so maybe she loves him a little."

"Perhaps." Rebecca pauses and rubs her hands together. "Poor fool." The sisters walk on in silence for a while, both dreaming their separate dreams. Sarah thinks of her little boy back at the cottage with her mum, maybe sitting up close to the fire, warming his hands, waiting for her to come home. She looks over at her sister, who is staring off at the frosted green hills that cut the sky. Sarah doesn't know what Rebecca is dreaming of but it is probably something more important, maybe world peace. Then Rebecca starts fumbling in her pockets again; she looks over at Sarah: "Do you mind if I have a cigarette?"

"Course not. Your hands are going to get cold, though."

Rebecca shrugs and takes one out, cupping her shaky fingers around the end to light it. She takes a long drag then frowns at the smoke appearing from her mouth like she doesn't know where it is coming from. "I thought I'd tell you before I tell the others. I was thinking I could announce it over dinner, chink my wine glass with a fork or whatever." With her cigarette between two fingers, she holds up a pretend glass and wriggles it about. "I've been offered this job in Colombia. I'd be reporting right from where all the action is." She brings down her pretend wine glass to her lips and takes another drag of her cigarette. Her eyes flit to Sarah. "Well, what do you think?"

Sarah frowns down at her father's bald head: they should have brought him a hat. "Oh that's wonderful, Rebecca." She blows her lips together. "It's just I was thinking of mum; she'll be so worried about you."

Flicking the end of her cigarette, Rebecca watches the ember melt into the ice. "Damn it, just be excited for me," she says, coughing into her fist. "Besides, mum's always worrying about us, whatever we're up to."

Raising her eyebrows, Sarah says: "You're only ever as happy as your unhappiest child."

"I suppose you understand all about that now, with little Charlie." Rebecca blinks and makes a half-smile.

"I suppose so." Sarah straightens her back a little. She hopes that her mum hasn't given Charlie too many biscuits, otherwise he won't be hungry for dinner. Mum is always doing that, letting Sarah be the baddie. "Do you think you'll ever want children, Rebecca?"

"Don't ask like that's a new subject." Finished with her cigarette, Rebecca flips it over her shoulder. "When me and Matt were still together we would discuss it."

"Well what about now?"

"My work is quite rewarding enough, thanks."

"Oh."

"I don't mean it like that; I think what you do is important too."

"Yeah, I know." Sarah stretches out her fingers and then grips them back into their dutiful position. "Dad seems to be getting heavier somehow." She glances over at her sister, who doesn't look back. "He's quite sweet these days; you could try getting on better with him."

"I have to remind myself that you're younger than me when you say things like that. Look, you didn't know him at his worst."

"Well he's a good grandfather now."

"I don't doubt it."

They walk on in a silence only interrupted by the slick of their father's wheels. Ahead, more mountains rise over the slate of ice; they are getting closer to safe ground. Then Sarah stops in her tracks. Staring down to the right side of the wheelchair, she says: "Look at this."

Rebecca moves closer and then goes down on her haunches to see the shadows darting about beneath the ice. "I suppose it's not fully frozen, then." With her finger hovered over the ice, she follows one of the fishes' movements. The chill that hums off the surface just reaches her fingertip.

Sarah tries to imagine life down there in the murky darkness. "It must be so strange for the fish to look up at the world through all that ice, like glimpsing a parallel universe."

A breathy laugh resounds from Rebecca. "I wonder if this means the ice is thinner here."

They scan each other's faces and then Rebecca gets up, shoving her hands deep into her pockets. Walking again, Sarah says: "Look – will you have a go at pushing dad? My arms are getting tired."

Rebecca pulls a face but takes the wheelchair. She strides along and pushes with force.

Sarah watches her sister and notes the fine lines across her forehead. Rebecca stares straight ahead with the dark concentration she's had since they were children. She's as lean as ever, too, and her elbows point out at right angles from the wheelchair. Around her throat a silk scarf is neatly looped and she has a small gold ring through one side of her nose that she didn't have when Sarah saw her last. Come to think of it, the last time they were all together was Christmas a year ago. Maybe that's how it is with them nowadays: they are just a Christmas family.

Sarah clears her throat and softly says: "You know I was watching a documentary the other day on all the cuts to legal aid, and they showed this debate about mercy and justice – it was between these two defence lawyers."

Rebecca purses her lips. "What made you think of that now?"

"I don't know. I thought it might be the kind of thing you'd watch."

"Yeah, I suppose."

The breeze pinching them, Sarah rubs her cheeks. "I'm trying to ask you which you think is the most important: mercy or justice?"

Rebecca starts chewing the left side of her lip and her walking speeds up. "Well mercy is important, of course, but justice comes first: it's what makes things fair."

Sarah looks up at Rebecca, who is quite a few steps ahead of her now, and sighs; she is sure the ice is too slippery to walk at that pace. "You'd be the first to say that life's not fair."

Rebecca glances back at Sarah but then turns to the front again. "No it isn't; that's why it's people's job to try and force some justice into it." In the distance, a pair of birds circles part of the lake as if getting ready to pounce on something, their wings beating heavily. Rebecca says: "Look, I'm amicable enough to dad; don't ask me to forgive him."

Sarah stares at her feet as she walks, watching the way they bob in and out of the white frame and searches for a way to speak her indignation. She was also at the dinner table when the plates were thrown against the wall. She too had been on that staircase when the shouting went on. But then there'd been the policeman at the door and their mum had listened with her hand against her cheek; a motorbike accident meant their father was in hospital for four months before he came home. Their mum brought his soup to his bed and fed him with a teaspoon.

Rebecca was old enough by then to make Sarah her dinner and take her to and from school. Sarah saw her once standing in the doorway to his room; just standing there, staring at him, laid out broken in his bed. When Rebecca turned round and saw Sarah, she walked straight off. It's strange; she still flinches from his touch today.

There's a clatter and Sarah's eyes snap up and skim over her surroundings. She takes in the trees only metres away. Her father in his wheelchair stands as an anomaly in the mass of white. There's no Rebecca. Sarah starts running but her feet slip so she stops and forces herself to walk slowly, dragging her legs wide apart. The crack lies centimetres behind her father, an aphotic gash trying to lick at his wheels. From it Rebecca's hand momentarily appears before being gulped back down. Sarah counts her breaths and gets down on her knees. Shaking, she drags herself along. At an arm's length away from the laceration and with shins soaking she calls: "Rebecca."

Crawling nearer, Sarah watches the fissures spread like veins beneath her. She reaches out and her fingers graze the water. Rebecca's head floats beneath, her short hair rippling the surface. "Rebecca!" Rebecca's arm waves up but like an ephemeral plant; fleeting, it falls, slapping the water.

"What the hell is going on?", their father calls out. Sarah stays silent and waits for Rebecca's arm to appear again. "Is this the hospital?". Trembling fingers fracture the surface. "I demand the answers!". Rebecca's arm swings up and Sarah grabs it and yanks. Rebecca floats towards her. "It's too damn cold in here." Sarah pulls harder but Rebecca is heavy and her body hits the edge. The ground quivering, Sarah lies still with her fingers wrapped around Rebecca's wrist; she caresses the bones through her skin. The shaking subsides and Sarah pulls again, managing to lift half of Rebecca on to the ice. "I'd like my dinner now," their father continues to shout into the silent air.

Her hands gripped around Rebecca's waist, Sarah inches them back across the ice, which lies underneath them as fragmented as a satellite image. "I asked for roast potatoes and turkey!". Sarah gets them a few metres away from the rupture before sitting back on her legs and wrapping her arms around Rebecca's stomach. "I don't want those damn potato faces again."

With Rebecca's hair splayed like seaweed against her cheek, Sarah squeezes until there is a cough. A stream of black water tumbles from Rebecca's mouth and her body shudders in Sarah's arms. Then Rebecca is still again, her head lulling against her chest and her arms stroking the ground. Sarah touches her cheek and rubs her arms and legs. She kisses the top of her head again and again: "Rebecca?"

Candice Nembhard

X

black men write black verse
their black words lead to a black hearse
(because they're) indebted by *the truth hurts*, or *real words*
many men face quick purse
salvaged on two-piece and green herbs
not finding the knowledge in the dirt
they recruit a new instrument to push
forth a serve
trigger warning when they shoot first
15-love as a sentence served and no
dialogue between a discourse and
interpreted words
Guilty assumed first
pressured by a gavel fist
made in slave terms
Thug replaces *negro* as a coded word
(but) a nigger's still a nigger
when he invents words
a nigger's still a nigger
when the words burn
in slick rap poem mixtape made-up passwords
that rest upon uneasy chests
like yellow birds
mining mama's blues
when the dust curls
speaking from beyond
in laymen's terms,
                    black
words

Freedom

America is run by fear
& its underbelly is full of repression
gurgling, ready to spout out its history, crying
we're sorry but the shit still stinks
and it's puddling beneath
America's feet, staining hard, swearing putrid
& pouring over.

Acne

I tried to squeeze the overhang & it
seeped out all over.
Crusting at the meet of a compound
substance;
protruding like an alarm
still ringing

Liam Offord

Alone, together

T HE CLOCK TICKS CONSISTENTLY, even though no-one can see it. The second hand skips around the clock, one dash at a time, as it always does. Reaching twelve it drags the minute hand with it while the hour hand settles itself two-thirds of the way. The clock awards itself a happy little ding for reaching 8pm on time.

Joy doesn't hear. She doesn't know how well the clock has done. She is immersed in a sudoku puzzle from 2010, printed on the back page of the *Guardian*. Joy holds the paper over her lap, staring at the puzzle while the front page picture of two smiling men, "David Cameron and Nick Clegg lead coalition into power", stares down at the floor. They can't hear the clock either, even as it ticks on, already committed to reaching 9pm.

Scribbling with a pencil that really needs sharpening, Joy finishes the top left box in her puzzle and takes a moment to read it over. She notices two fours have snuck into the same row. Maybe they just want to stay together, or maybe they are trying to ruin her puzzle. Joy doesn't care. She moves to rub one of them out. The rubber is too worn down so Joy only smudges the excess four. The error has unsettled her; she decides to go over her work.

Joy taps each slot in her puzzle to check for mistakes, unwittingly matching the rigorous ticking. For eighty-one seconds the two form a harmony, tapping and ticking their way through the evening until Joy reaches the end. The two fours hiding each other was the only transgression that slipped through; she has control again now and plunges on, looking for a hole that can be filled. The clock ticks on; it's too dedicated to marking each second to give up.

Puzzling her way through the sudoku, Joy is oblivious as a car pulls up outside. She is unaware of the engine's low grumble and the ensuing silence. She doesn't hear the car door slam shut or the footsteps rattling up the driveway followed by keys being thrust into the front door. Joy looks at her puzzle and the clock ticks on, even as the door opens and her husband stumbles into the room, tripping over the threshold.

Joe gathers himself and closes the door behind him. He pats his tired suit, trying unsuccessfully to smooth out a crease. The light is off; Joe sees the smooth, complete black outside the window and feels the darkness sitting heavily in the room. He wonders how long Joy has been sitting like this, not registering the light leaking out of the room; he wonders how she can even see the paper she is looking at. The window looks out on to nothing, until Joe closes the curtains. Who knows what the window can see now? The room slips into a glum greyness. Joe wants to help.

Maybe it's because he feels guilty.

He flicks the switch on the lamp. A splash of light trickles over the sofa from underneath the lampshade. The darkness still lingers about the room, Joe notices, but at least Joy can see her puzzle a little easier. His wife doesn't look up and her husband stands motionless, unsure what to do.

At last, tortured by the paralysis, Joe leans down and kisses his wife gently on the forehead.

"Hello," he says. "How was your day off?"

Joy ignores the affection. It has come far too late. She fills in another number on her sudoku. "Are you late, Joe?"

"Sorry?"

"Late, Joe. Are you late? I can't see the clock."

"Oh!" Joe looks across to the mantelpiece to check the time; he always forgets the clock is hidden now, ever since Joy placed their wedding photo in front of it. The clock ticks on.

He checks his watch just in time to see 19:59 shift into 20:00. Joe's watch isn't as committed as the clock behind the photo.

"Yes, I'm a bit late." He doesn't reach the apologetically nonchalant manner he was reaching for when he says this, too sheepish. "I had to work late." Joe doesn't know why he lies.

"Again?"

"Huh?"

"Again, Joe? You had to work late again? That's been the case a lot recently." Joe waits a second; he expects Joy to say more. She doesn't. The clock ticks on, resolute, and Joe's watch limps along, unable to catch up. He shuffles past Joy, squeezing between the sofa and the coffee table with an old newspaper on it. Joe glances at the headline – "Libya: rebels move government to Tripoli" – as he sits down. Joy's legs are on the sofa and Joe can't find the room to get comfortable. He looks at his wife but she doesn't want to look at him. The two sit for a moment, Joy immersed in her puzzle and Joe wedged in. You couldn't say they are sitting together, it simply isn't the case; they just happen to be on the same sofa.

It is Joe who breaks first. He jumps out of his seat and moves to the table near the window, shifting a pile of newspapers off the chair so he can sit down. Joy yawns. It's not the type of yawn that comes about from tiredness, not the yawn that drifts, languidly, towards bed. It's a pointed yawn, shot straight at Joe. Joy yawns and then goes over her puzzle again.

Joe sits with the tired suit still clinging to him. He should have come home hours ago and taken his suit off. Instead he's been… elsewhere. The tie around his neck is heavy, pulling Joe down. He loosens the knot a little but doesn't remove it, even though he wants to. Joe watches his wife, sitting on the sofa in front of him.

Joy fills in the last number on her puzzle. It's a three. Looking at her completed work, she doesn't smile but rests the paper on her lap. She keeps her gaze forward, away from Joe. The room is very still, she realises. It's almost stuck. As if the world just forgot about this little room and dropped it somewhere, leaving Joy and her husband to live out eternity.

If Joy listens, of course, she would know this isn't the case; she would hear the little clock ticking on behind the wedding photo, dragging Joy and Joe through time on its own, pulling them along through their lives with nothing more than a rhythmic click and a happy little ding every hour. Joy doesn't hear any of this; all she can hear is the silence spreading itself, filling every corner of the room. Joe can hear the silence too and they sit together, each as unhappy as the other, and the clock ticks on but nobody listens.

Joe breaks first again; he has to speak or the silence will strangle him. "I'm sorry, you know." He really is; he's desperate to atone. In the end, his apology falls far too short, "I'm sorry I had to work late."

Joy hears her husband's lie and decides not to respond.

"I really am sorry… it's not like I find any joy in it."

Joy feels a small, sardonic laugh tumble out. Her husband, her pathetic and foolish husband, has found one more way to upset her.

"You don't find any joy in it?"

Sitting there, with the tired suit pulling him down and his wife still looking anywhere but at him, Joe realises he shouldn't have spoken. Her laughter circles around his ears and finally, far too late, Joe wonders just how much Joy knows.

"Do you know this sudoku came out in 2010?" she says.

"Pardon?"

"2010! Don't you think that's impressive?"

Joe frowns at his wife, Joy doesn't see.

"Think about it, Joe. This puzzle came out five years ago. That's a long time. Do you think it's been easy being a sudoku puzzle all that while? I'm sure it's wanted to try something else – maybe it's thought about being a crossword, or a word search even. But somehow, five years later and it's still a sudoku puzzle! It's really very impressive, Joe. Five years and it hasn't changed. Hasn't given up being a sudoku puzzle. That's commitment."

Joe sits motionless in the exhausted suit. He stays there as Joy turns, at last, and looks at her husband. Joe looks at her blue eyes, though the light is so poor he can barely make them out. Joy looks at her husband, as worn down as her pencil, and wonders how anyone could see him differently.

Joy turns back.

"2010, Joe. What else was going on then, can you remember?"

Joe's eyes jump to his wedding photo on the mantelpiece; he didn't want them to but that doesn't seem to matter. It is impossible not to stare at it. Joy's eyes are much clearer in the photo. He always thought photos faded after time, but in the murky room Joe realises it is real life that fades.

She knows what he's been doing. That much is obvious now. Joe looks at the photo for a long while. He wants to stop, he wants to get up and sit next to his wife but he can't; it is far too late. He keeps his focus on the photo, which looks down on him with smiles and feeling and hopes that are long gone. It's just a mask now, happy to sit there and pretend, obscuring the clock and all the reality it brings with every little tick.

"Joy, I– " he gives up, two words in. There's nothing to say. Joe can't fix his mistakes; he can't just rub them out. He looks down at himself, on the seat, and then back to Joy on the sofa and knows it's permanent.

"You really shouldn't leave me alone all day to solve puzzles, Joe."

Josh Patterson

Shadowman

THE OLD MAN WAS OUT WALKING across a long white beach, the sea off somewhere behind him creating a faint rushing sound and his wife beside him so that there were twin footprints in the sand as they made their way. She did not quite have a face but that didn't matter.

Neither said anything but the old man felt that she was happy and that he was happy as well. They took pause to watch the sun go spinning off across the sky and for it to become night and the old man felt her hand leave his but he did not look around to watch her go. Then he began to walk by himself.

He came upon a bar somewhere out there and made smalltalk with the people there for a time. They were all of them laughing and joking in loud voices, and the sound of them mingled with the smoke from their cigarettes and filled the air up. There was only one at the very back who was still and silent. He was stood up against the wall in shadow but the old man felt that he was watching him. He craned his neck to get a look at him but then the walls began to crack and break and crumble away. He glanced behind him as if he might find his friends still sitting there but they were gone, and there were only the heaps and piles of torn-down roads and the great jittering shadows of broken buildings. He picked a way at random and began to run and eventually his family called him over as they could see he was distressed. They gave him a sandwich and held him until he had stopped crying. After a while he felt as if his wife should be there to share in the food too so he got up and went looking for her, walking out over the fields and calling her name until he'd left the picnic far behind and everything had become a dense forest. He racked his memories but could not remember having ever been there before in his life.

Still, it was beautiful, so he went on and admired the new place. There was no wind and not a sound and the old man found it peaceful and soothing with the trees tight all about him like he was some king that they were charged with protecting. Eventually however the trees opened out and made a clearing for him and the old man saw that there was a small house in there, wooden and windowless and rotten with creepers crawling all over it. Again he could not remember ever having seen it before.

Inside it was much the same as out. There was a large ornate rug lying on the floor but it was all covered over with dust and soil and the furniture that was not lying broken in the corners of the room was shabby and faded. There were picture frames hung on the walls but they had no pictures in them. A chandelier swung up high on the ceiling, a good ten feet above the old man.

He walked on through long corridors and into rooms that didn't make sense to him. It was as if someone had taken fifteen different houses and put them all into a box and shaken them and then tipped them out again. There was a room so full of old gramophones that the old man had to edge along the wall to get by them, and another that looked like it had been lifted straight from the nineteen-twenties except that there were big flat black screens on all the walls. He found staircases that went nowhere and doors that led back into the room he'd just come out of, and he went on and on through them until a shadow stopped him.

It was up high on the wall dancing about. Laughing. It said that it had been watching him go through the rooms and it asked him if he was lost and if he needed help. The old man looked around the room he'd just come into and saw that there was nothing in there but a small wood fire that was burning steadily. I am lost, he told the shadow.

The shadow's head bobbed a little as if it was nodding. It moved and danced at all times in the light of the flames, and it was difficult to tell exactly what it was a shadow of. It looked like it had arms and legs like a human but its head was not the right shape. It was longer and thinner. I could tell that you were lost, it said, the words echoing around in the old man's head. You have been dreaming for a very long time.

This worried the old man. How long have I been dreaming? he asked, but the shadow would only say, a very long time, a very long time.

Then the shadow told him, I know the way out. Back into familiar land. But I am going to need something from you. I am going to need a bit of you to take away with me because I do not have a body or anything of my own. After you give me that I will let you go.

The old man turned away from the shadow. He tried all the doors in the room in an attempt to escape but there were just walls behind all of them, just the bricks. None of them led to any other room or anywhere. When he turned back around the shadow seemed to be watching him patiently, still doing its little dance. If you don't give me a bit of you I will keep you dreaming.

The old man took a breath and tried to be brave. He squared up to the wall that the shadow was on and told it that this was his dream and his own head and he would not be controlled within his own head.

The shadow shuddered and moved along the wall as if it were trying to get a look at him from behind, but the old man turned so that it could only face him. This is not your head, it said eventually. You wandered out of there a long time ago and now you are in a different part of the dream country. The part that I own. So if you do not give me a bit of you to have I will keep you here. You will not wake up.

The shadow didn't say anything more but waited until the old man had checked all the doors over and over again and pounded on the walls. It waited until he was finished and had slipped down on to the floor.

Which part do you want, the old man then asked. The shadow came around the wall to be beside him. Give me your voice, it said. You don't even use that any more.

So the old man did. After that the shadow could speak out loud. It sang as it danced along the walls in the light of the fire and the old man could do nothing but look on. After a while the shadow stopped and seemed to remember that the old man was there. Then every single door in the room opened, and the shadow watched and laughed as the old man threw himself through the nearest one and started running again.

But the place was still a labyrinth and the old man found himself as clueless as ever within it. No door led out into the forest by which he had entered. Or none that he could find.

Eventually he entered a room with a large wooden wardrobe engraved with small roses similar to one he remembered having as a child. He used to hide inside among the musty old fur coats and either someone would open the door and he would jump out or no-one would find him and he would fall asleep. In an odd way this small familiarity comforted him. He sat down and tried to speak, or cough, or make any sound, but nothing would come up out of his throat. Only soundless air. He pounded on the wardrobe once, to prove to himself he could still make some noise.

When the shadow arrived it spoke to him as if he were a child. Couldn't you find your way? It asked in a clumsy sing-song. Oh dear, oh dear, oh dear!

The old man knew it was toying with him and enjoying itself. He wanted to cut the shadow off, to shut it up. To hear his own words and his own tunes that he used to sing in the old days thrown back at him by no mouth at all was torture. I thought you'd be able to find your way. I don't know if I can even help you! I thought you'd be able to find your way.

What will I have to give it, the old man thought. What will I have to give it for it to show me the way.

The shadow crooned low and swayed along the wall.

Let me see, it said, as if it had heard every word inside his head. Your eyes.

The old man quickly got better at bartering. He kept the things he felt he would need until the last moment. His feet, his sense of touch. The things he needed to escape. His teeth, if he needed to fight his way out. He massaged his hollow chest. He regretted trading his eyes. But there wasn't anything he could do about that now.

When he moved about the house he was positive it had gotten smaller. Now he knew the layout of the rooms intimately, he could tell when one disappeared. Each time he traded with the shadow the house got a little smaller. Fewer rooms, fewer doors. But still no door that led out, yet.

As the shadow's body grew with each part the old man gave it, so the house shrunk.

It couldn't even really be called a shadow any longer. The old man had begun to hear it moving about in rooms next to him. It had scraped along the walls when the old man had given it his hands and now most of the wallpaper was ripped and hanging off in strips. He didn't know when exactly the shadow had pulled itself off the wall. When it had stopped needing the wall. But he didn't think that it could stand up yet. When it came to speak to him its voice was from below. Near the floor. Maybe it dragged itself along with his hands. He thought about it and was actually quite glad he had given his eyes away.

It would find him and speak to him often. Sometimes it would just tell him things. About the places it had been, and the things it had seen. The dark, broken cities. It was all a game to it, he thought. That it would eventually steal all the pieces of him away so that there would be nothing left.

I am this house, it said. Did you know that? I run through the brickwork like blood. Every moment you are within these walls you are within me.

The old man never wanted to listen. But it was in his head. He couldn't block it out. It would eventually ask for another piece. Last time it had been his lung.

Sometimes he thought about asking how long he had been dreaming. But he was afraid to know the answer.

Molly Ellen Pearson

Game reserve at dusk
S 33 32.175
E 26 07.117

Blue air tinged with amber,
cricket song, the kindling scent of trees.

The rangers parked and left the four-by-fours
idling under their light sweat of dust.

I walked back to my hut to shower
in water gravid with a day's heat,
the showerhead a bucket punched with holes.

The rooftops mellowed into veldt.
On the verandah the tame cheetah,
collared like an awkward dog,
lay with the sun on his shoulder.

Grasses fell against the horizon,
sparse and yellow as unbrushed hair
on the back of your neck.

I had almost forgotten how to miss you.

The bends
N 5 57.990
E 116 00.821

Ebb tide drew us from under the ocean's skin
    finned and slick.

As city lights reprised themselves
    in the bruised waters of the bay,

we forced limbs out of our cracking spines
    – but lungs were harder.

That was the day you taught me oxygen,
    its rosary of molecules,

until I could feel it, yellow and astringent,
    flowering in my blood.

There are depths from which you cannot ascend
    more than once in a lifetime:

amphibious yearning, the feeling
    of drowning in landlocked air.

Patrick Peel Yates

Palimpset

Retrod, deep seated
Neo-urban desire
Castles pressed in moonlight
Skim across eyelines
Like crayons on a penny stencil
So many visions compacted
In a whistle: GO!
And they're off,
More this time
And more, and more;
Velvetine soldiers plodding
Axes aloft, lances sharpened
Ready to prick the sun and eat its fire.
The pavement lit with carcasses
And the air suffused with wonder
Wonder at all this
Holy noxious perfume, spinning
Outwards, always,
Backwards
Forwards
Orbiting the one thing
You never, ever see.

For every time a bell rings,
An angel gains its wings.
For every time a horn sounds,
Another hits the ground.

Louise Pigeon-Owen

The wish

THE PRAWNS ARE TIRED AND WITHERED. My spoon guides them through a sea of mayonnaise. I don't think they want to swim anymore. Some of them have even jumped to the safety of the lettuce. I hear crying but it's not Michael. He always cries silently into his handkerchief. Sometimes the tears roll down his nose and hang under the tip like ripe plums. The sound is coming from the other side of the room. Loud and screechy like the crow that got trapped in our chimney. A little girl is screaming and hitting the table with her fists.

"I want chips and ketchup," she says. "And I want my cake."

Her mother says that the cake is for later. The girl yells and throws her chicken at the window. It leaves a thick, greasy splatter. Michael's plate is empty and he is picking dirt from under the nail of his thumb with a knife. He's been doing it since I gave him that Swiss Army knife for his tenth birthday. Back then he was a rosy little thing tottering around in ripped dungarees.

In the summers he would turn the mandatory sunhat around and flatten the cap so he looked like a baseball player. He hated sun cream and would run away shouting "Poison! Poison!" whenever I tried to apply it. Even after bribing him with sherbet lemons or strawberry liquorice, he would inevitably wipe it off on his T-shirt, leaving stains that could never be washed out. He used to have dark circles of dirt on his knees from digging to find moles and rabbits. He had a cowlick of blonde hair which refused to be combed out and never-ending scraps of fruit peel between his teeth. Now he smells of lavender and is immaculate like the tablecloth.

"It's my birthday next week you know?"

"No mum, it's today."

I say nothing. He is scraping under the nail of his index finger now. The ragged lines on his brow are like the furrows of a ploughed field. He used to love playing with his toy tractors. When I look down, the plates are gone. *Did I finish the prawns?* A waiter returns to pour Prosecco. The cork makes a bang and the chair wobbles beneath me. I hold the table so I don't fall. The rising bubbles make faces and stick out their tongues. Luke drinks his but I just watch mine. The knife changes hands and he scrapes under the other nails. I feel full. Fit to burst. But I haven't eaten much, so my stomach can't be full. Too late, I feel warm liquid flow into my knickers.

"Luke…"

"It's Michael, mum."

"Michael, I needx…"

But the sea bass is here and he's ordering mineral water. I eat. The skin is crinkly like tin foil and the flesh is soft but has no taste. The milky fish eye is turned up at me and I think it winks. Its mouth is open and I waggle my finger inside, feeling the small teeth and wet lips as it kisses me. Michael's skin is waxy and red but mine is flaky and soft like the fish's. The plate is hot and I trace the edge of it with a finger like an orbiting planet. Round and around. Clockwise then counter-clockwise. He says I should eat more.

"This place isn't cheap, you know."

But the bones poke out all fierce and the bass looks angry so I decide to leave it alone. I inspect the napkin spread across my lap. It looks like a net trawling the ocean. I lift it up. In it I have caught some prawns. There are green beans trapped there too.

"What are you doing? Put that down. Christ's sake – people are staring."

"I didn't want the prawns to die."

"They're already fucking dead."

"Sorry."

He sucks air through his front teeth and asks for another napkin.

The water is poured, making gulping sounds, like the glasses are drinking it themselves. I think of his thirsty little mouth back in those hot summers. Sipping from his blue beaker as I rocked in the hammock. Rocking the heat away. Lazing through a John le Carré novel. A glass of freshly pressed apple juice nestled in the tangled goosegrass. The trees were bent in towards each other as if sharing a secret. A couple of wasps had clambered into the glass and were drowning in the sticky liquid but I just flicked them out with the straw. Other wasps paddled through the sultry air, drunk on rotten apples. Everything back then seemed thick and sluggish. Even the wind took its time as it sauntered through the leaves.

Did Michael say something? Impossible to tell because he's still looking down at his nails.

A girl is carving faces into the table with her knife. Savage eyes and mouths in the varnish. Now she shoots peas through her straw at the other diners. Each bullet makes an angry farting noise as it leaves her gun, like a car exhaust back-firing. Pffttt, it goes. Pffttt pffttt pffttt.

A pea appears in my palm. I blink and roll it around. I let it travel down my life line but it stops half way down. I bite the inside of my cheek. *That can't be a good omen.*

A little girl is grinning at me. All tooth gaps and gleaming gums. I smile back.

"Please stop playing with you food, mum. You're not a bloody kid."

Michael nods at a passing waiter.

"Yes, we have everything we need, thank you."

The waiters twirl between chairs and tables like spinning tops. Keeping track of them all makes me dizzy. I try to count them but the numbers slip through my fingers like eels. *Are there nine? Or maybe seventeen?* They're carrying piles of clean plates and dirty dishes and glasses and menus and bills, all with a look of confusion. Perhaps they have no idea at all what they're doing. They just whizz from one place to another, and suddenly I have to grip the table because they're moving impossibly fast, so fast I can barely even see them.

"Happy Birthday to you, Happy Birthday to you…"

Things sharpen and I feel less giddy.

At a table near us, a family sings out of tune. Another confused waiter threads through plush seats holding a white cake topped with dangerously lopsided candles.

"Make a wish!"

I wish I was young again and it was summer and I was wearing my polka-dot dress and my crumbling straw hat and Michael was chasing butterflies with his net.

"What did you wish for, honey?" an anxious mother asks her daughter.

"A million pounds!"

I pull a bone from between my teeth. *How did that get there?* I look at François' shoes poking out from under the table. You can see the whole room in those shoes. The faux gas lighting and sickly flower-print wallpaper, warping as the shadow cast by the tablecloth shifts across them. And there's the other diners, upside down and twisted. Oval eyes and sharp dagger teeth. And everyone's laughing. Laughing and laughing and clinking glasses and leering and gulping and slurping. After some time, the noise becomes a different type of silence. I focus on the shoes. Beneath the thick polish is a vortex and dad calling my name.

"François, I need the toilet."

"Can't you wait until the end of the meal? I've ordered lemon drizzle cake, your favourite."

"Thanks." My tone is flat like the wine in my glass. *Doesn't he know I hate lemons? Or is that oranges?*

"And it's Michael. I don't even look remotely like François."

Michael's biting the skin around his nails which has peeled loose. A nasty habit which he developed when the bullying started. It's the one thing which betrays his carefully cultivated appearance. He pulls a strip of skin back, revealing the bubblegum-pink flesh beneath. A berry of blood surfaces and he sucks on it.

"I know we haven't been close these past years," he says to the bleeding thumb, "but I wanted to say how grateful I am to you for all that you did when dad passed away. I hadn't thought about how hard it must have been for you, raising a child all by yourself. Especially when I wasn't even yours…"

He pauses to tear off another line of skin. "… and I'm sorry for the way I've behaved over the years, I really am."

Why can't he let the past go? Why is he digging it all up when the dust has finally settled?

I take a loose thread from my jumper and I waggle it about until it comes free, pulling out a whole row of stitches as it goes. Each unravelled stitch is a sheep bouncing through the meadows. *Are they leaping with joy or running from something?*

The wetness has seeped through my woollen tights and is dripping into my trainers. *Did I knock my glass over? But it's warm, it can't be water.*

I say I feel ill so we skip desert. Michael deliberates over the bill. He counts every item and adds up the total in the margin of the receipt to check that he hasn't been scammed. *Is he doing this to spite me? Showing how I'm not worth a penny more than absolutely necessary?*

He takes even longer pondering how much to tip.

"Five pounds, do you think, or should I round up to six? I can never remember if it's ten or fifteen percent in this country. No, five. The service was passable but not fantastic."

The tea lights have almost burned out and the setting sun trickles through the windows, casting us onto the wall like shadow puppets.

A little girl near us has finished her cake and is stealing fistfuls of her brother's when her parents aren't looking. When he starts to cry, she pinches him hard on the arm to make him stop.

We stand up to leave. An electric current ripples up my spine and I clamp the table edge hard so I don't buckle. Recently the pain has been getting a lot worse. *I really should tell Michael.* Before I can speak, he points to my chair.

"What did you… oh my God, you haven't just… Jesus Christ, mum!

"Why are you shouting?"

"What's wrong with you? You're like a baby, pissing yourself in public, it's disgusting!"

I look down and see that my seat is soaked through.

Michael grabs our coats and escorts me out sharply. He pushes me so hard in the lobby I fall. But I don't bounce back up like he used to when he was little, showing off his bruises like war medals. I stay down.

Michael jams his arm under mine and drags me from the restaurant, his cheeks flaming red like telephone boxes.

"What a fucking nightmare," he says as he stuffs me into the car and straps me in place with the seatbelt. "I wish I'd never taken you out in the first place."

I wish I wish…

Although I can't remember, I know that the wish was important. And as we whizz away I cross my fingers and hope that it comes true, whatever it was.

Jake Reynolds

On the Bewdley sweet chestnut invading you

I.

Swiftly into postboxes – coach windows – high-rise
        offices and art studios
        long and eerie, a dismal thrill
        a tendril in a ruptured drum
        an oil spill in brazen light
kaleidoscopic, your innermost thoughts
gifted in knowing a liar
from throat to boot
the memory of your grandmother
a flash of brilliant silver in her garden
with a level tray on which a jug of ginger beer
and tumblers in a pyramid made summer summer
        in the corner a tentacle waving at you
        to – I don't know –
        "face the music" – "meet your maker" –
an idle man tossing a bag of seeds to obese birds
        your politics is a tree in autumn
        your love is blight, or unsent letters,
swiftly out of postboxes they lurch – vomit in reverse –
the tapping at the pane on the journey
passing the Severn
your father in an office block,
        computer wires   his fate.

II.

There they are in the grey blazer
then you on your walk with them in the grey cold
when you made a joke and they said
  Dude, I don't think that's a thing
  and you felt "yea big"
look at my lowest branch
grooved into the dirt
one of my cousins groomed the top of your head
they pointed up and said
  blossom
you loosened the Martenitsa from your wrist
your Bulgarian flatmate gave it to you last year
you looped it around a grinchy twig
you didn't say a thing
you wonder if they'll end up renting art studios
in one of the world's tallest cities
  there's nothing off about all this
  your face is a chink of streetlight
  through the curtain
  you blame it on your sleeplessness
  and the dust motes make Braille
  I just reach out and feel you feel

III.

Round here the squirrels get vertigo
and fatly hop away with nausea
     think of coming home
     and the furniture rearranging
     at the speed of the clock,
     a scabby coffee cup lurching in contretemps
     in the centre of it all
everybody you have ever known has reached a rung on me
if you squint hard enough you see their names
like the game you played last Christmas
     the higher you climb the worse it gets
I know you are here for the sunlight
     drumming fingers, cluster headaches:
     things I shed in spring
     poor adornments
what a grim parade
every unborn thing has seen me
plugging the womb
with a voice, svelte, like this,
almost weeping when you are upended into the air –
isn't the air a terrible thing
a bladed, ugly, smartarse thing –
I lower my mouth to a puddle or river
to get some of you back
     but really it is not in my nature
these things will not desert you until you are old
and in senility think –
washing away the grit of a careless family
at the kitchen sink –
that you have cracked it
     you will never crack it
     it is already lost to you

Jessica Rhodes

the old house

on Google Maps when you
type in the address of the old house
it looks like 2006 maybe
because the white Rover is parked outside
and your mother can be seen with a
blurred-out face and a
full black bin bag in one hand
lifting the dustbin lid with the other

and six years later she is
standing there still indefinitely

boxes

as a way of saving money, your mother drives to
all the McDonald's around and collects their boxes.

on one of the boxes your mother has written "China" in marker pen
and you record this on Facebook because your brother has pointed out

that it is a pretty impressive feat that we have managed
to fit the whole of China into a cardboard box.

(11 Likes)

shrine

it switches places and sits in the underpass
with flowers in a beer glass vase
on a piece of fabric and a note
by someone who wouldn't usually handwrite but does because
telling someone
 even though they don't have eyes
to read it
        wish i had done more n
        it will be different next time
is important

Zein Sa'dedin

Oriental

aladdin dreams of occupying
the land between my thighs
of having me as his brown genie
bottle belly dancer bowing to
his every wish yes master
anything to please master

aladdin paints my arabian nights
black like the oil he bleeds from me
counts my eyelashes like jewels
habibi make me a magic carpet
I could bury your body in it

Earth

Wildfire you wound me touch me
turn me over my aching self my parts
downside right upside left you rid me
of my breath deoxygenate my death
bed I accept my dependence on your
déjà vu tongues uprooting my past
and searing off the last layer of skin
Wildfire you bleed me from within
like a leech you suck out all my
toxins mutilating my acres until
mother nature heals my wounds
with holy water
Wildfire for weeks you annihilate
everything I live for force me to start
over but now rest so I can make the
best of your destruction and rebuild
the world you disrupt again

Seven years of silence

After I left, I would unroll my "r"s every morning,
train my letters to lie flat against the bottom of my mouth.
I would smoothen out every syllable,
soften my "s"s and speak in a slow drawl.
I would practice my "p"s in the bathroom mirror,
careful not to crack it with my accent.
I would rinse the guttural "d" out with mouth wash
and force myself to love the emptiness between my teeth.
Before I left, I would recite Darwish every evening,
and watch my teta fall to the floor five times a day in devotion.
She told me Arabic is the mother of poetry,
counted her prayer beads ninety-nine times a night with our names.
She painted pictures of Jerusalem's olive trees,
showed us the scar she carries on her wrist from a broken fence.
Two weeks after I left she died of a collapsed lung
and since then my tongue has become a foreign entity.
I've forgotten how to make it speak of her.

Resurrection

Give birth to
the Dead Sea
in December
and the Jordan
will fall to its
knees in prayer.
Kiss her lips
and suffocate
yourself in her
salt and she
will carry you
slowly to the
surface three
days later.

Starry, starry

Dear Vincent held
the weight of the
North Star on his
shoulders, let its
dust sink into
his fingertips,
and devoured
the stellar sky.
Dear Vincent said
there is no blue
without orange,
so he sliced his
skin to give us
the bleeding sun.

Sarra Said-Wardell

Contact

Neither of us agreed to keep
in touch but today I would like to be someone
else's fingers holding open your mouth,
mostly because I am waiting
for the brutal architecture of October
and thinking about tongues.
The other reasons are because you called
and it is my birthday and I am drunk.
Meanwhile, in Birmingham
there is a woman who wakes up
in bed every morning knowing
that somewhere in the blue blanket of sky
little green men are desperately
trying to reach her.

Rachel Sammons

Blowfish

W E CALLED IT BLOWFISH. I remember lying flat on my back and calling to my dad from upstairs.

"Blowfish! Blowfish!"

He thudded up the staircase and charged into my bedroom, eyes filmy and bloodshot from staring at the computer. I would squeal as he threw up my shirt, pressed his face into my tummy, and blew. He blew a blowfish. He blew a loud, trumpet sound. It was a pleasant, ticklish feeling that filled my body like ripples of water. I kept asking him to do it.

When he wasn't blowing blowfishes, he was at the computer desk with his fingers sweeping across the keys. Unless I said I wanted to tell him something. Then he would halt and cock his head at me and say, "I'm all yours." It was a very special to thing to have my dad all yours. He made people frustrated because he only gave them part of him, or none of him. He waited in the car after church and the Deacons' wives called him boring. They needed him to say funny things or teach boys' Sunday school. They told me I could talk to their husbands if I ever needed anything.

When I was fourteen, Andy asked me on a date. He had gelled hair and he made homemade yogurt because the store-bought ones did not have the healthy bacteria needed for his body. Mom loved to play with his hair and come up with vegetarian dinners for him. When we crowded the table, Andy led us in prayer. Dad stared at him with glazed-over eyes. He usually loved to pray.

When Andy broke up with me, I cried in bed. My hiccups blew snot into my throat. Dad sat at the edge of the bed because he didn't want to be the type of dad to rub my shoulder or side-hug me. I had to help him out.

"Blowfish my arm, daddy," I said.

So he blew a blowfish into the fleshy pillow of my forearm. I heard the bloated, bugle sound and stopped crying.

I dated a lot of guys in high school and dad liked none of them. One of them, Michael, got a part of dad, one time. Dad showed him how to make a spreadsheet on Excel. But then Michael wore a suit to the first family dinner and dad exhaled loudly whenever he looked at him. Afterwards, I said to dad:

"Can I ask you something?"

And he said, "I'm all yours."

I broke up with Michael. I blew a blowfish on my own arm because dad wouldn't pity me enough to do it. It didn't feel the same, though, and I wished dad could always be all mine.

I was eighteen when I first saw Rob. He had stringy, shoulder-length hair and he smiled sadly at me as if I was a homeless person. He helped dad paint the garage and I could tell, glancing out the window, that he was trying to keep up a conversation. But maybe dad's not all yours until you ask. Dad just grunted at his paintbrush and swiped his forehead. I snickered because Rob didn't know how all my past boyfriends failed.

But Rob was curious about God so dad let him come with us to church. Once afterwards, Rob said:

"Quick question – about Jesus dying for sins and stuff – um…"

Dad looked him in the eye and said, "I'm all yours."

I was blown away.

But all that glided into a halt when one day, dad told us that he had to move.

"For my job," he said, "I have to go to Beijing."

"Can I come with?" I said.

But I knew.

I had college to attend and the American life to live. I would stay here.

That night, I cried in bed until dad heard, blustered up the stairs, and blew hundreds of blowfishes into my belly, my arms, my cheeks, and all over. The sound was a wheezing gust and it flowed more tears to my face.

Summer flushed by in a sweep of hot air and nightly blowfishes. A week before college, Rob drove Dad and I to the airport and we said goodbye with no hugs or kisses, just my teary gaze to rival his red-soaked, computer-wasted eyes. Rob shook his hand and Dad said he would pray for him.

A few years later, I'm still Skype-ing my dad. It's difficult because there is a huge time difference and his schedule runs at a gasping, non-stop pace. But I still hear from him through email sometimes.

When I visit my friends in Fargo, I see Rob in a bar that sells hamburgers for one dollar. He buys me a drink and we get flushed-cheek tipsy. He's funny, sometimes, when he chooses to be. I can get hiccups laughing at him.

He did it to me one time. It was on the bridge at nighttime and snow fell in silent puckers. I could hear Rob's breath, clogged with congestion. I swore we would kiss but instead, he plastered his lips to my neck and blew. He blew a blowfish. I was blown shocked out of my skin. I wondered if his dad ever did that to him.

My dad was right about Rob and everyone else. It's a big deal to be all someone's. I don't give all of myself to any boy now, only one, the one who deserves it. He's the one to steal my breath away.

New year

January 1ˢᵗ, 2020

"You're through to Mars division, how can I help?"
"Oh, hello. I'd like to apply for the programme."
"Great, I'll just pull up an application form. What's your name?"
"Frank Stevens."
"Age?"
"Twenty-five."
"And why would you like to apply for the programme, Mr Stevens?"
"You're looking for people to die, right?"

February 2ⁿᵈ, 2020

So this is what the inside of NASA looks like. I suppose all their money must go towards spaceships and not interior design.

I sit down. A woman enters the room and sits opposite, lays her clipboard on the table and looks up at me. "Mr Stevens?"
"Yes."
"I'm Doctor Brown; I'm here to do your psychological evaluation."
"OK."
"How are you feeling today?"
"Fine."
"If you're feeling fine, why are you volunteering?"
I laugh. "It's not that simple."
"So explain it to me."
"I don't want to."
"What do you know about the programme?"

"I know enough."

"Stop avoiding my questions, Mr Stevens. It doesn't look good in a report."

She's too sharp for me. My mind is slow these days. "I know that myself and a few other volunteers will be put in a spaceship and —"

"Rocket," she interrupts.

"What?"

"You'll be put in a rocket. Spaceship is a bit science-fiction."

"Right. So, we get into space and head towards Mars to test the new rocket and see if it can sustain humans for that long. There's a ninety-nine percent chance it will be unsuccessful. But it'll make for some good data."

"So if you know all this, why are you volunteering?"

I shake my head. "It's a long story."

March 23rd, 2019

Harry puts me on another group project at the office. This is my third in a month. I don't know why he thinks I'm so good at them.

I'll be working with Carlos and the new girl. She got here last week, can't even use the photocopier. I think her name is Lisa; I don't know, I haven't actually met her yet.

I walk into the conference room and they're already sitting down, having a chat, Carlos with his romantic wavy hair tucked behind his ears, Lisa with a ponytail. She looks up at me as I walk in and smiles.

"You must be Lisa," I say. I sit down next to her. "I'm Frank."

"I've heard a lot about you, Frank," she tells me. "You're apparently quite a legend at group projects."

"Well, I'm the only one who knows how to use Excel."

"I can use Excel," Carlos says. This is a lie. I've seen him use Excel. The only thing he knows how to do is make the cells different colours.

"Shall we get started?" Lisa asks me. "The presentation is in a week, after all."

"I think that's a good idea," I say.

"Me too," says Carlos.

March 30th, 2019

I catch up with Lisa outside the conference room after the presentation. We had successfully, with the use of many pie charts that Carlos did not help with, advised the company on the most fiscally sound ways to market a new type of soap.

"That went well, I think," Lisa says when I approach her. She has her hair in a ponytail again, like she does every day, long and brown and straight, swishing from side to side with the slightest movement of her head. We walk towards the water cooler.

"You were great," I say.

"So were you." She grins at me. "I think they were impressed by the pie charts."

"Well, as a group project legend, and a proficient Excel user" – she starts laughing before I've even finished – "I know that pie charts bring the house down most of the time."

"Most of the time? I don't quite understand that statistic when you put it like that. Do you think you could make a pie chart for me?"

"Yes. I think I could manage that."

"Maybe you could give it to me later."

"Later?"

"At the pub down the road after work."

"Oh, we're going to the pub after work, are we?"

"Yes."

"Carlos too?"

She shakes her head, ponytail landing on her left shoulder. "No, I think he's too busy reading."

Lisa points to Carlos, reading Microsoft Excel for Dummies under his desk. I laugh so hard that water comes out my nose. Lisa takes a picture of it.

After three drinks I tell her, "I love your ponytail."

"Thank you," she says, smiling hazily like people do when they're tipsy.

"No, I mean it."

"I didn't think you didn't mean it."

"I mean it! I have a thing for girls with ponytails. I don't know why."

"Maybe you fancy horses?"

"Stop making jokes. You'll make my beer come out of my nose."

"I refuse to stop. We could make a collection. 'Drinks Coming Out of Frank's Nose.' Open a gallery, make a fortune."

"You think snobby art critics will like close up photos of my nostrils?"

"We could say it's modern art. The tragedy of being a grown-up means you never laugh. Here is a man recapturing his youth."

"Through his nostrils."

"Yes."

"All right then. Make me laugh."

I take a sip of my beer, keeping my eyes locked with Lisa's. Pale brown, crinkled with her smile and laughter lines. She lifts her arm to her mouth and blows a raspberry. I laugh harder than I have in years, because I'm tipsy and it's childish and I've finally found a woman I'm excited about being with.

June 14ᵗʰ, 2019

"Happy birthday!" Someone is standing behind me with their hands over my eyes.

"Who is it?"

I feel their body press against my back, feel kisses on my neck.

"Carlos?"

She snorts right next to my ear, so loudly that I start laughing too. Lisa takes her hands off my eyes and turns me around so she can kiss me.

"Did you get me a birthday present?"

"I thought I could just have sex with you. Save myself some money."

"Cheapskate."

She opens her bag and pulls out a box covered in wrapping paper. "Here. Happy twenty-fifth, you old man."

"You're twenty-five in a year," I tell her as I tear the present open.

She shakes her head. "No. I'm going to be young and beautiful forever. Open your present."

It's a toy spaceship.

"Ah, I see. You're telling me to go back to my home planet because I'm such a horrendous boyfriend I must be an alien."

"No! It's to recapture your youth. I feel like that's a theme in our relationship. Don't you feel like that's a theme in our relationship?"

"I thought the theme in our relationship was love."

"Oh."
"Yeah."
"I love you too, then."
"Good."

August 30ᵗʰ, 2019

I put the spaceship on the mantelpiece in our new flat. Lisa pays for the pizza and we sit on the floor and watch Netflix because the sofa and the TV are still in storage.

"I've never rented anywhere before," she says, having just moved out of her parents' house. "Can you paint the walls?"

"Depends whether the landlord likes the colour."

"We should paint the walls. They're too beige."

"What colour?"

"Red and green. The colours of the first pie chart we made together."

I snort and push her shoulder with my foot. She pushes back. We wrestle and make love on the carpet.

October 4ᵗʰ, 2019

"How was your first day?" I ask Lisa when she gets home from her new job, assistant to some prolific journalist. She doesn't want to work in soap marketing forever, after all.

"Good. Sofia, the woman I'm working for, she's lovely. She was nice to me when I messed up her coffee order. That's Marcus' job now."

"Marcus?"

"Her other assistant."

"Why does this woman need two assistants?"

"She's very busy and important."

"I can't imagine being too busy and important to make my own coffee."

Lisa rolls her eyes.

October 20th, 2019

"I looked in the newspaper for computing jobs."

"Looking to change careers?"

"Don't look at me like that. You have a first in computer science, you shouldn't be stuck making pie charts."

"Pie charts are what brought us together."

"Well, we're together now, so you can stop. There's a job going on the floor above mine, some tech support company. Do you want me to ask if they'll give you an interview?"

"Whatever."

October 25th, 2019

"How did it go?"

"I didn't get it."

"I'm sorry."

"That's OK. I'm kind of relieved. I like where I am, you know? I like the people I work with."

"You never stop complaining about them."

"I stop sometimes. Anyway, how was your day?"

"Good. Got put on a group project with Marcus." Her hair falls in her face. I can't see her expression.

November 11th, 2019

"There's a Christmas party at the office next week. Do you want to go?"

"God, no. I don't want to see any of those people again."

"It might be fun. We could make fun of Carlos again. He's trying to master Publisher now; won't stop putting Word Art on things."

"I don't want to."

"Lisa."

"I'm working that night, anyway."

December 1ˢᵗ, 2019

"Do you want to do anything for New Year's?" I ask Lisa while we read in bed.
"Get drunk," she says.
"Anything else?"
She doesn't answer.
"Lisa?"
"There's a party at my office."
"Oh, OK. We'll go to that then. It'll be nice to meet some of these people you talk about all the time. What's that guy's name – Marky?"
"Marcus."
"Yeah. It'll be nice to meet the guy who's spending so much time with my girlfriend."
"What's that supposed to mean?"
"Nothing."
She turns off the lamp and we are plunged into darkness.

December 5ᵗʰ, 2019

I find a receipt for a suitcase in the bin. Lisa hasn't expressed a desire to go on holiday. I want to ask her about it, but I forget.

December 7ᵗʰ, 2019

I get home from the Christmas party at 11pm. I told everyone I had to leave early because I didn't want to leave Lisa alone. But she's not back yet.

December 10ᵗʰ, 2019

"Now Simon, how many volunteers are you looking for and what things should they consider before applying?"
"Well, Nick, we're looking for about six volunteers in total. Over twenty-one, in good health, with some kind of scientific degree, computing or physics. Applicants should be aware of the risks of the programme – to be blunt, if you are chosen for this mission, you probably won't return."

I turn the radio off.

December 21st, 2019

"Are you going home for Christmas?"
    "No, why would you ask me that?"
    "I found a suitcase under the bed."
    "So what?"
    "You didn't have a suitcase before."
    "Leave it, Frank."

December 25th, 2019

I wake up on Christmas morning. I've been looking forwards to this for weeks, my first Christmas with Lisa. I got her a Lego set, one that builds this huge spaceship. I thought it would be funny, fill in the serious silences that are becoming common.

    I turn over to her side of the bed and find nothing but an envelope with my name on it.

December 31st, 2019

I know where Lisa is right now. With Marcus at her office. Getting ready to kiss him when the countdown reaches zero, because Marcus has ambition. Me? I haven't changed in the nine months we've been dating. She heard from the floor above that I'd not shown up to the interview. She'd found her Christmas present under some coats in the wardrobe and started crying because I wanted to stay exactly where I was forever and she wanted to grow and change.

    I finish off the bottle of wine and make my New Year's resolution.

Adrian Southin

Dover strait / Dallas Road beach

The ocean is so different here
more brown than blue
opaque and thick
as steamed milk
sea foam raking
each stone
in froth and film.

It does not sate
the thirst for
my Salish Sea.
I could drink
the viridian lip
of the waves
their ripples mapped
like lines eroded
into skin; the fibrous edges
of driftwood rank
with brine and crab shells
hollowed by crows and seagulls.
I could drink that coast
until my hands swell
my stomach distends and sloshes
and the salt puckers my body.

The Doves of Victoria station

The pigeons are missing
their toes; digits reduced
by disease, incest
or the crush of a shoe heel.
One hobbles by
on two fat stubs,
plumage ingrown
and moulting.

One, a dove
(if not for the granite
tail and covert feathers)
has no left foot
white tufts ending
at a bare pink joint,
the right the only
fully formed foot
in the station.
Picking at flakes
of a fried pastry,
the pigeon walks
under my suspended boot.

Cambridge

Dear Vincent held
the weight of the
North Star on his
shoulders, let its
dust sink into
his fingertips,
and devoured
the stellar sky.
Dear Vincent said
there is no blue
without orange,
so he sliced his
skin to give us
the bleeding sun.

Adam Vale

Clan

B RUCE LEE DIED SUDDENLY IN 1973. He took a pill for a headache and it burst his brain. Greatest fighter in the world, movie star, cold-blooded killer, and he got mugged off by an aspirin. See, Bruce used to be able to do this thing on set. I saw it in a documentary. He would practise his kicks all the time, firing his legs right past the crew's heads in faux hits. He was so good, so powerful, he could even tickle people's ears with his toes when he did it. One time a crew member moved their head at the last second and Bruce hit him full force in the face by accident. I think they quit their job after that; chunks of white teeth, split gums running red. I wish I was there to see it, just so I could have learned first-hand.

The gang is out practising kicks in the garden today. I'm lying on my front on the flat roof of our bungalow as I watch Johnny and Lou fight on the spiked grass. They shoot clumsy sides and roundhouse blasts at each other, scarring the air. I can smell the baking heat of asphalt waft up around my chin, feel my naked torso grill against its itchy surface. Johnny is my little brother. I taught him to fight just like dad did me before he left; how to throw a real punch that can kill a guy. Lou is the neighbour from across the street who's a little older. We met him when we moved here. He's bald and has a nose ring, says he likes punk music. I don't know about all that. I do know he likes scrapping, though, and we've got to be friends over the summer by giving each other big peach black eyes.

I watch as Johnny misses a hit and stumbles, slips into the cracked mud. He tries to roll but isn't fast enough, gets caught by an elbow to the ribs. He yells out in pain and mom cranks open a window.

"Calm it down, boys!" she yells, tired breasts practically hanging off the sill. I don't think she gets dressed very much these days, prefers to smoke inside her room and listen to old records with a nightgown on. Poor girl.

Lou holds up his hands as Johnny writhes on the floor. "Sorry Mrs. C," he calls. "We're only messing."

"Well, you keep it that way. And thank you for mowing out front, Lou. Very handsome work."

"Any time."

They hold each other's gaze for a moment, saying things without saying. Mom blushes. The window slams. We all relax.

I slip down from the roof and land with a wet thud. We store petrol cans up there, buy in bulk to save a bit of money, and some of the stuff has leaked all over my legs. I wipe my shorts down, motion to Johnny to go fetch me a drink. He hobbles into the house with sweat leaking down his face.

"Gotta be faster, kid," I tell him, patting him on the back.

Lou stalks over to me. We've been practising for most of the morning, slugging at each other and twisting knees so that all our joints click with each step. "Conditioning", we call it. If you can give a hit you've got to be able to take a hit. Not like that guy on the film crew who quit after just one knock. No way. Sometimes we even hold each other by the arms and take smacks to the gut. It makes us tough.

"Listen, Buddy," Lou says to me. 'You still got old Gibbin's cat?' He's referring to a neighbour of ours, a crazy witch who lives right up on the corner. Often we steal people's pets, see, for our habits. I've been keeping Gibbin's kitten in a box under my bed and feeding it cornflakes since we grabbed it last week.

"Sure I do," I answer. I throw a spear-like jab at him for fun and he ducks. "Why'd you ask?" "Thought we might set the bitch up in The Ring."

The Ring is a little fort we've built in the back of Lou's garden. It's made of chicken wire and corrugated iron from a dump a few streets away. It's not quite big enough for a person to stand in. Instead what we do is put Lou's dog in it, a blind old Rottweiler that he's very fond of, and we set the mutt on whatever bum we can find: rats, hamsters, ants. We say "Trigger, sick enemy," and he goes for the thing. He almost always wins, leaves the cover of the battlefield a popped cherry red.

"Sounds good," I say. "This evening?"

Lou nods, sits down on a little deck chair by a radio and turns it on. The noise and hum of crickets from a nearby wood gets drowned out by hard rock. "This evening it is," he says, and snorts a line of coke off the crook of a bruised thumb. Lou's that kind of guy.

Johnny and I decide to walk over at dusk, only I pop in to see mom beforehand. Knock lightly on the door. She's sleeping on her bed. A book is folded across her chest and a full ashtray teeters dangerously. A glass of water on the side, paper coaster round and swollen. The room stinks of smoke.

"You OK?" I whisper.

No reply.

I walk over and carefully slip the book on to the floor, place the ashtray on a chest of drawers. One of the shelves is open slightly, a money clip balanced on the corner. The shelf is full of lingerie and crisp silver condoms. I frown and close it, cross back over to the bed and cover mom with a blanket. Johnny calls for me from downstairs. I go to him, shutting the door gently, and we leave.

Lou's adjusting The Ring with a hammer when we get there. I walk up behind him and imagine snapping his neck with my bare hands, imagine breaking him and then pissing all over his corpse in defence of my family. I fire a kick off and try to nick his ear, end up jarring a button of his spine.

"Jesus, Buddy!" he yells at me, scrambling to stand. Lou's green eyes flash at me and he raises his fists.

I grin stupidly, say, "Sorry."

He rubs his spine and curses. "Come on," he mutters. "Let's get this over with."

It takes all three of us to lift Trigger into The Ring, puffing in the gloom as the sun sets. We balance him on the edge, his thick gut a cushion for the spikes, then tumble him all the way over. It takes the mutt a few seconds to get his bearings. Then he promptly falls asleep again. Lou goes over to the ice box in the corner, grabs a cattle prod from the top of it. He stabs the dog twice in the back to make it wild, and then we throw in Gibbin's kitten from a box we brought with us.

Trigger sniffs. The white patch of discolouration near his nose twitches.

"Trigger, sick enemy," says Lou. The command is full of love.

The dog barks once, twice, leaps. He grabs the kitten straight between his big white teeth and chews as if it's soft tobacco. It doesn't even have time to squeal, just lies limp and lets its cranberry bags of guts slip out on to the ground. We cheer and dance around The Ring. Trigger waves his head back and forth to celebrate the kill and sprays us all with blood. Some of it lands on my cheek and I bring a hand up to feel it. Runny and fresh. I dab a little on my finger and taste it. The sour drink of champions. My tongue laps up a few more drops and I tell Johnny to do the same.

"Same again tomorrow?" I suggest, thumbing my nose at the dead cat. It's still folded in the hollow of Trigger's jaw.

Lou unwinds a hose from the wall and washes down The Ring. Trigger twists in the white water like a fat cobra, full and happy. "All right," Lou says stiffly, squinting at me. We leave him to clear up and head home to bed.

That night I lie staring up at my wall. Bruce stares back at me from a fighting stance and faces the door from a poster. He's my protector. He guards me as I drift backwards into the pillow and wait for sunrise. He's always there. One day I'm going to be just like him. I'm going to be a killer fighter way stronger than any man alive; join the army, go rogue and hunt the bad guys then make movies about it. That's my plan. That's the plan that drums me to sleep below the moon.

There is a loud slam that jolts me upwards. I hear the front door go. Someone is leaving the house, or entering it. Carefully and without making a noise I tread my bed and peer out of the window. I see a nightgown darting across the road. It stops at Lou's front door, ripples like a ghost. The nightgown knocks and Lou answers. They embrace, and I blink the sleep out of my eyes.

A few moments later two figures appear as silhouettes in another room. The curtain slides away to reveal spread brown buttocks rammed against the glass. I fall back into my covers and hold back a scream. Green eyes loom at me from the darkness. I cannot sleep now. Rage trembles inside of me. He never said. Never thought. And she. How I cared for her.

Silently I rise from my room and slide past Johnny's sleeping lump. I slip on my trainers and break free of the door, only to run outside and climb up on to the roof. I look over and see that the silhouettes have moved on to a bed, so I take one of the big red petrol cans and lump it down to the ground. I check the street, then cross and bring the heavy liquid with me on instinct. I feel sick.

Trigger is snoozing quietly in the shadow, locked on to his chain. There is a thump from Lou's bedroom and a rapturous moan and I tug the dog awake. Revenge is white hot, gives me strength to heave him with all my might and push him over the wire. Trigger lands, looks up at me with milky blind eyes and sniffs. I pat him softly, bring up the petrol can and douse him in it. He whines and barks, but I go on dousing. What a pleasure it is to douse this ring and the summer behind it, to soak it in petrol smell. I pour a small trail over and away in the grass, a kind of fuse.

The cattle prod is still on top of the ice box. I take it and conjure sparks. My work lights with a whump, consumes the fuse and then The Ring. Trigger starts yelping loudly. I smell his fur and flesh singe and cook, melting into the ground where the cat still lies. The banging from Lou's room has stopped.

He and mom appear in the garden and he sees what I've done, charges at me. But, like Bruce, I lash out lightning fast. He folds neatly over near the flames and mom shrieks. I grab her by the wrist and drag her home. I lock the door. She says nothing. I say nothing. Johnny sits in the kitchen.

Snap. The kick went *snap* and Lou crumpled. It keeps playing out on my eyelids in glorious red as cars pull up outside. I was just like Bruce. Lightning fast. Dying young.

Nathaniel Josiah Ming Yu Woo

What they don't understand

Lily

M Y MOTHER IS A WHITE LADY. In my head, she has Cinderella's hair and Snow White's skin. Her voice sounds beautiful, in my head. She never stutters or fumbles her words because her tongue knows how to move in just the right way – it doesn't get caught between her teeth like father's. No, my mother's words are perfect. They listen to me and they tell me things and they make me feel special. When my mother speaks, I *am* special. I know I'm special because I'm the only one who can hear her voice, and when I do, I feel her words chirping around my tonsils. It soothes me. When she whispers and rolls her "R"s, I imagine that she's hugging me. And I like that. I like the feeling of a hug, and I like my white mother. I *love* my white mother. In my head, she loves me too.

Father never tells me who my mother really is, why she is gone. When I ask him, his wrinkles stiffen and his eyes shout at me. It's a subject he wants to ignore, but I don't know why. Shouldn't he love her?

The only thing he tells me is that she is white. He can't ignore that. Nobody can. Customers always stare at me. It's hard not to see how light and brown my hair looks under all the red lanterns, and my skin looks so pale beneath my uniform: the same bright red qipao Mama Julie wears. With Mama, it looks normal, but with me, people raise their eyebrows. They don't expect to see such a white girl packing Chow Mein into silver containers. But Joseph says it's always been that way. People have been giving me looks since the day I was born.

"The only difference is that they used to spend all day talking about how cute you were," Joseph says.

"But they don't do that any more, big brother. Now they just think I'm weird."

"That's when you just have to ignore them, kiddo. People always feel threatened by what they don't understand."

*

Listen. I want to tell you a bit about Joseph, because after my mother, he's the most important person in my life. He's my brother, but he's 15 years older than me and we look nothing alike. We have similar noses (fat little buttons with no bridge), but that's about it. I could never call him "Joseph" to his face. He's so much older than I am, it feels disrespectful. But he doesn't say *my* name either. I'm "kiddo" to him, not Lily. It should make me feel small, but when he calls me kiddo", it just makes me feel comfortable.

Joseph doesn't have a white mother like I do, but he does have a real mother that he can touch. She's a Chinese lady, but she's very dark, almost brown. Long face, tight bun of strict black hair, and a constant catfish-frown on her lips. She makes me call her Mama Julie. She doesn't live with us in the takeaway, but every weekend she comes to work with us, cook us some dinner, and hate me. I don't know why she hates me, but she does. Whenever we meet, she greets me with the same words: "Oh, pretty little girl getting fat, huh?"

I used to hate it when she said that, but now I just think of the words Joseph told me. People always feel threatened by what they don't understand.

But Joseph *does* understand me, mostly. I can't feel his words in my throat, but I can feel them stretching my brain. Joseph knows things. My big brother *knows* things. More things than anybody. The only reason I can say I love Joseph is because he taught me to understand love. Before then, I didn't get it at all – it kept treating me differently each time I saw it, kept smiling at me one day and frowning the next.

"Love has its own emotions," Joseph said. We were in the kitchen, cleaning up after a late shift. Joseph was holding a mop, wiping dried sauce from the floor, while I swept pieces of diced garlic and spring onion with a dustpan and brush. From out front, we could hear father slamming cupboards and moving chairs along the ground, so we tried to speak quietly. "We all have our happy loves and our angry loves, but that doesn't stop it from being love. You understand that, don't you, kiddo?"

"Yes, I understand *that*," I said, "but, big brother, your angry love isn't the same as father's angry love. How can two things be the same when they're so different?"

"Well, you know how some people can be Chocolate People, and others can be Kitten People?"

I nodded my head.

"Well, kiddo, Chocolate People are always gonna give you Chocolate Love. And when that Chocolate Love is good, it's always gonna be sweet and delicious. But when it's bad, it's gonna make you feel sick and greedy and ashamed of yourself. You know what I mean? Kitten Love's always gonna be cute and playful until the day it decides to randomly scratch you."

"And what about everybody else? What other types of love are there?"

"Loads. An unlimited amount. Too many to describe."

"OK," I said, "But what about father? What kind of love does he give?"

Joseph rubbed his eyes and chuckled.

"Oh, kiddo. You ask some difficult questions."

"It's OK if you don't have an answer."

"No, no. I have an answer. I've thought about this a lot." Joseph knelt down and placed his great big hands over my shoulders. "Look, kiddo, you probably won't understand this, but our father's love is medicine. It is. It might taste foul, and you might not want it, but it will make you better. You can trust me on that. father's love is nothing but medicine."

Joseph

Yes, I suppose I did tell her that our father's love is medicine. Bit of an odd comparison, I know – slightly cheesy – but it made sense at the time. What you have to understand is, when you talk to Lily, you need to speak to her in a way that will actually touch her brain. She has a unique mind, one that's made from skin rather than words or letters. She will feel even the smallest thought, and the smallest thought has the capacity to tickle her or soothe her or cut her or bruise her.

It makes sense that she thinks that way. Words don't mean anything in our house. Just look at the way our father runs the takeaway; he has a million different hand gestures and facial expressions to direct you with, but no words. He'll simply mime a stirring motion at you if he wants you to prepare the sauce, or chop against his palm to say: "Go cut the vegetables." The only words I've heard him say in the kitchen are the numbers on the menu.

But look, I've been studying my father for a long time and, by now, I've sussed out all the different things he says in his silence. I'd consider myself an expert. I could tell you my father's mood, just by listening to the way he sharpens his knife (the blade will hum if he's happy, hiss if he's mad), but that doesn't mean I expect Lily to notice all the same things. I don't expect her to notice how much his lips quiver when he shouts at her. She's just a kid. Hopefully she'll understand one day, but sometimes I do wonder. She spends a lot of time in her room, whispering under her breath, talking more to her imaginary friends than she does to anybody else. That's why I told her that our father's love is medicine – she needed to know how good his love can be, how vital.

Lily needs to know a lot of things. She needs to know about the smile on our father's face when he first brought her home. She needs to know how many times Mama stayed up crying, feeding her and rocking her to sleep. But more than anything, she needs to know about herself, about where she came from. I need to know where she came from too. When we first took her in, I tried asking mama and father about it nearly every day, but I always got the same reply. "The hows and whys don't matter. All that matters is that she is here."

But come on, look, I'm not dumb. I've never really cared about how or why. I've only ever cared about who.

Mama Julie

Not me. Not mine. Though she taste milk like mine, slept in arms like mine, stop crying only when Mama Julie say hush hush. Not mine, though I named her, gave her who she is. Lily. Little white flower.

She came from the other one. The tall one, the red hair one with small speck of sun on her cheek. My head pictures that woman well. The first time we meet, I see her walking around church with her knees together, her hand in shape of praying, greeting everyone with "God bless" like good Christian woman. Such a good Christian woman until the day she take my husband and anoint him with the smell of her.

I never know why he do that, why he hurt me when he say he love me. *Love* me. You don't share love with other woman sheets, don't share what's mine. I tell you what's mine: his love mine, his face mine, the smoke of his stubble mine, the scar between his thumb and finger mine, the chocolate mole on his cheek mine, his children – every children he have and ever have – *all* mine. Everything mine if he love me, everything his If I love him.

But he broke our everything when he had that other one. I was going to leave straight then, take Joseph with me, but then he say that the other one is pregnant. He take my arm and he say "please, please, please" and "sorry, sorry, sorry", but I don't forgive. I only forgive when I see my little white flower. I know I have to stay when I look at her, because in her face I see toothless kindness. Teardrop eyes that sparkle and say they need me.

So I forgive as long as I have to. Stay as long as I have to. Treat her like mine, raise her like mine, until Joseph old enough to take care of her. Then I let go, just before she remember me. Visit just to see her and push her away, call her fat, ugly, pretend I don't need her. Otherwise it hurt too much.

Lily, I love. Joseph, I love. It hurt not to see them every day. But I have to let go. Have to. Not me. Not mine.

The father

"It's yours," she said down the phone. Her voice was shaky, cracks biting at the ends of her words. She told me she didn't want it, the child. She talked about the shame, the sin, the reasons she had to leave and hide and forget herself. But she said the child would be born, no matter what. "I won't kill it. We've sinned once already. You'll just have to raise it yourself."

I said yes. When she invited me to her house, I said yes. When she asked if I was comfortable, I said yes. When she touched me, when I felt her skin, I said yes and yes and yes. So, when she asked me to raise the child, there was nothing left for me to say.

The moment Julie found out, about everything, she said no. First in a whisper, then in a shout. Then she said nothing but tears. Then she left and there was silence.

There's a Chinese proverb: "Water and words are easy to pour but impossible to recover."

Impossible to recover, the tears and the yesses. I've learned to say nothing.

*

When you say nothing, you start to notice things. Recently, I was out front, closing down the takeaway, when I overheard two people chatting in the kitchen. Walking behind the counter, I placed my ear against the door. It was Lily and Joseph. They were speaking quietly, but I could just about hear the croaky rumbles of their voices. As I tuned into their conversation, I heard Joseph chuckle and start to speak.

"Our father's love is medicine," I heard him say. "It is. It might taste foul, and you might not want it, but it will make you better."

The words made my heart feel thick in my chest. Medicine: it will make you better. I wanted to tell Joseph he was wrong. My love could never be medicine, could never heal, never recover. My love could only break things: the family, Julie's heart, Lily's light-skinned face. My love was illness. My love was water and words, poured so easily into the wrong place, in the wrong way. And now it was irrecoverable.

So I stood, and I stayed silent.

Biographies

BLYTHE ZAROZINIA AIMSON is a third-year English Literature with Creative Writing student. Her dissertation is an exploration of Tarot cards and their connection to poetry, from which her poem La Grand Mère is extracted.

ERIN BASHFORD is a first-year English Literature with Creative Writing student. Originally from the Midlands, she now lives in Norwich.

MATHILDA BEAUMONT EPSTEIN is 20 years old and was born in London. She is a second-year English Literature student who has only recently started discovering her love for creative writing after completing a module in it this year.

Born in Bedfordshire, LIZA BLACKMAN is a first-year English Literature with Creative Writing student at UEA who runs purely on enthusiasm, coffee and company. She is most passionate about comedic writing and LGBTQA+ fiction. Presently she is working on producing several short stories focusing around people and the way they interact with others.

CALLUM BROWNE is a second-year English Literature student from a small seaside town in Kent. He studies, when no other option presents itself, at the University of East Anglia, is a connoisseur of own-brand Tesco wine, and reads mopey existential philosophers in his spare time because "they're the only ones who really get me".

GABRIELLE CORRY-MEAD is an up-and-coming writer from London Town. She works with the fantastical, the comical, the tragical and the downright mad. Her work has been included in several anthologies and potentially an independent e-book depending on how well she deploys her publisher-wrangling skills. She hopes you enjoy her stories; they were written for you.

HELENA CUTHBERT is a second-year English Literature with Creative Writing student at the University of East Anglia. She is from a small village in Nottinghamshire where she lived most of her life and she currently lives in Norwich. Primarily, Helena writes poetry and script.

CATHLEEN DAVIES is a third-year undergraduate. She loves creative writing, she plans to move to China and she can say the alphabet backwards.

NOAH DE GRUNWALD is a second-year creative writing student, originally from London. He enjoys writing songs, fusing dancing with karate, and wishing he looked like he did a few weeks ago. His poetry can be found @saturdaytowers on Tumblr.

GABRIEL FLYNN was born in 1991 and grew up in Manchester. He is a student on the English Literature with Creative Writing BA.

ALISON GRAHAM is a writer who also volunteers for Amnesty UK. She's been commended in Foyle Young Poets and has work forthcoming in *Fur-Lined Ghettos* magazine. Her debut pamphlet is due in 2016, with Pyramid Editions.

REBECCA GRAHAM is a London-born second-year English Literature with Creative Writing student at UEA. She is an aspiring scriptwriter and author and her past work has also been selected for the 2015 Undergraduate Anthology.

LAWRENCE GREENLEE, formerly known as Kate, is a third-year in English Literature with Creative Writing. He came out last year as a transgender man and has been writing about his experiences in the form of comic books, poetry and transgressive fiction.

FAYE HOLDER is a final-year English Literature with Creative Writing student. Her story was inspired by the frustrations she has felt as a dyslexic writer struggling to capture and organise her thoughts into coherent sentences.

JULES IGNACIO is a Swiss-Filipino undergraduate doing English with Creative Writing at the University of East Anglia. He likes long walks on the beach and watching cheesy rom-coms. He's easy-going and laid-back. He's received a scholarship for his writing and has been published under different pseudonyms. But those works are a past he's trying to forget.

LUKAS KOUNOUPIS is a third year English Literature with Creative Writing student, hailing from Athens, Greece. He enjoys writing prose, is horrible at anything involving poetry and would like to design video games in the (near) future.

FRANCESCA KRITIKOS was born and raised in Chicago, Illinois and currently studies English Literature with Creative Writing at the University of East Anglia in Norwich, England. She is a columnist for *Moloko House* and her poetry has been published in *Witch Craft* magazine, *Alien Mouth, Lighthouse, Little River* and more. You can find her on Twitter and Instagram @fmkrit.

PATRICK LALLY is at home in Northampton and Norwich. He enjoys Thermos flasks and Anglepoise lamps.

AUDREY KING LASSMAN is a first-year student from north London. She likes fictional characters and aspires to create them for a living.

KATHRYN LEIGH is a first-year studying English Literature with Creative Writing. They have been published in student magazine *Octarine* and are really excited to appear in the wndergraduate anthology! Aside from writing, they enjoy inclement weather and wearing clashing patterns. They are sustained by a diet of tea, toast and the macabre.

SHANNON LEWIS was born and raised in Mexico. She is a first-year English Literature with Creative Writing student at the University of East Anglia. She was recently published in the student-run magazine *Octarine* (which she also runs, but that's not important). She has been known to write short stories, the first drafts of poems, and ideas for scripts she will "finish one day".

Born in London, raised by his parents and childminder, BENJAMIN EI LUBBOCK is in his final year studying English Literature with Creative

Writing at the University of East Anglia. Although this is his first official publication, his first work of prose was finished at the age of nine at sixty thousand words.

ADAM MARIC-CLEAVER wants to be a writer, but won't be. He will probably end up working in admin for a large sock manufacturer. His only ambition at the time of writing is to listen to "Surf's Up" by The Beach Boys. His story, *The Propeller*, is dedicated to Ronnie O'Sullivan.

Originally from London, ISABEL MARTIN is currently studying English Literature with Creative Writing at the University of East Anglia. She spends approximately 95% of her time reading and has an unhealthy obsession with 80s music and Harry Potter.

HARRY MENEAR is a first-year English Literature with Creative Writing student. He writes short stories, bad poetry, and has started at least five novels. He runs and edits *Octarine*, a literature and arts periodical at UEA. One of these days he might actually get around to writing the second chapter of a book, but he doubts it.

SARASWATHI MENON was born and raised in Chennai, India. She's a final-year Film and English Studies student and hopes to write films someday. She aims to challenge the Orientalist perception of India as she voices the concerns of new age India in her writing. You can access her writing, photography and art at saraswrites.tumblr.com.

CIARA MORAN is currently in her second year studying Literature and History at UEA. She loves to write stories in her free time. She also has a keen interest in exploring the world of children's fiction.

JENNY MORONEY was born and raised in London and is currently an English Literature with Creative Writing student at the University of East Anglia. She mainly likes to write short stories and poetry.

CANDICE NEMBHARD is a poet, artist and short-story writer from Birmingham. Her first short story *Kaleidoscope Eyes* was published in 2012 by The Gentlemen's Press. She is currently in her final year of the BA English with Creative Writing programme at UEA. Alongside her academic studies, Candice is an keen traveller and editor-in-chief of *Underpass*, a Norwich-based publication showcasing literary and art work from the region.

LIAM OFFORD was in last year's version of this anthology. All his friends are sincerely hoping this doesn't start going to his head.

JOSH PATTERSON originally hails from Northern Ireland, but decided to swap the green pastures and Guinness for concrete walkways and Snakebite at the University of East Anglia. Though the English Literature with Creative Writing undergraduate course he is enrolled in often pleads for some nice sensible work about real human beings, he just keeps producing creepy little ghost stories and the kind of dark fairy tales you probably wouldn't want your children to read.

By day she is MOLLY ELLEN PEARSON, writer and responsible tea-drinker. By night she seeks out the dark forces and joins their hellish crusade.

PATRICK PEEL YATES is a 20-year-old writer from Hackney, north London. He studies English Literature with Creative Writing at UEA as a poorly veiled front for his forays into the Dark Arts and in his spare time enjoys triceratops. (Yes, the plural is triceratops; he enjoys that too.) He claims to understand what gravitational waves are but it's pretty clear to everyone at the party that you can't "surf them to the centre of the universe, man". Main sources of inspiration include garlic bread and Leo's Oscar speech.

When LOUIS PIGEON-OWEN isn't sleeping, binge-watching or buying fabulous shirts, he rather likes writing film reviews, short stories and poetry. He enjoys all things surreal and macabre and hasn't written a happy ending since 2009.

JAKE REYNOLDS has had poetry published in *Far Off Places*, *Hark* magazine, *Vademecum* magazine, *Cuckoo Quarterly* and others. He currently writes poetry for *The Norwich Radical* in response to current events. *On the Bewdley sweet chestnut invading you*' is written after, and inspired by, the works of T.S Eliot.

JESSICA RHODES writes poems and plays. She is co-founder and president of UEA Publishers and has work forthcoming in *Alien Mouth*.

ZEIN SA'DEDIN is a second-year English Literature with Creative Writing Student. She is from Jordan in the Middle East and a lot of her poetry is about exploring the implications of the Arab identity.

SARRA SAID-WARDELL was born and raised in London and is currently a second-year student of English Literature with Creative Writing at the University of East Anglia in Norwich.

RACHEL SAMMONS was born in Fargo, North Dakota and has lived in many different places. She has graduated with a degree in English Literature and Creative Writing. She co-writes a blog about personal stories and issues in the world of Christianity at tallgirlshortgirlblog.wordpress.com.

FIONA SANGSTER is a first-year English Literature with Creative Writing student at UEA. She writes short stories, poems and screenplays. Someday, using her passion for dialogue and bad jokes, she hopes to be a screenwriter for television and films.

ADRIAN SOUTHIN is a Canadian poet, fiction writer and filmmaker on exchange from the University of Victoria in British Columbia. His work has appeared in *SubTerrain*, *Plumwood Mountain* and *The Warren*, among other publications.

ADAM VALE is a first-year undergraduate at UEA. A writer and poet, he divides his time between Norwich and the Cambridgeshire area.

NATHANIEL WOO was born and raised in Essex to an English mother and a Chinese-Malaysian father. He discovered his love for reading and writing when Dr Seuss taught him the difference between one fish, two fish, red fish and blue fish. Thanks to this early education, Nathaniel is now one of the world's most respected authorities in the field of differentiating fish by their number and colour.